Twayne's United States Authors Series

Sylvia E. Bowman, *Editor*

INDIANA UNIVERSITY

Harvey Fergusson

TUSAS 257

Photo courtesy of Alfred A. Knopf

Harvey Fergusson

HARVEY FERGUSSON

By WILLIAM T. PILKINGTON

Tarleton State University

TWAYNE PUBLISHERS

A DIVISION OF G. K. HALL & CO., BOSTON

Library of Congress Cataloging in Publication Data

Pilkington, William T
  Harvey Fergusson.

  (Twayne's United States authors series; TUSAS 257)
  Bibliography: pp. 157-62.
  Includes index.
  1. Fergusson. Harvey, 1890-1971—Criticism and interpretation.
PS3511.E55Z85   818'.5'209   74-34319
ISBN 0-8057-7157-3

MANUFACTURED IN THE UNITED STATES OF AMERICA

To Betsy

Contents

About the Author

William T. Pilkington was born in 1939 in Fort Worth, Texas. He was reared on a farm a few miles south of Fort Worth, and his early education was in the public schools of several North Texas communities. He received his Bachelor of Arts degree from the University of Texas at Arlington in 1961. Texas Christian University later awarded him both a Master of Arts degree (1963) and a Doctor of Philosophy degree (1969). He has taught at Southwest Texas State University and at Texas Christian University. Currently he is Associate Professor of English at Tarleton State University in Stephenville, Texas.

Dr. Pilkington is the author of a pamphlet (*William A. Owens*, published in 1968), a book (*My Blood's Country: Studies in Southwestern Literature*, published in 1973), and nearly two dozen critical articles and reviews. His main scholarly interest is the literature of the American West and Southwest, and many of his articles and reviews have appeared in journals such as *Western American Literature*, *Southwestern American Literature*, *New Mexico Quarterly*, and *South Dakota Review*. He is a charter member of both the Western Literature Association and the Southwestern American Literature Association. He was recently elected to the Executive Council of the Western Literature Association and, since 1973, has served on the Editorial Advisory Board of the journal *Western American Literature*.

Preface

I first read Harvey Fergusson's books because he is a writer from the American West and I have long been interested in the literature of that region. I lingered over his works, however, because the best of them—several of the novels in particular—seemed to transcend the obvious limitations of much Western writing. In both his fiction and his nonfiction he raises complex issues and problems that are not quickly or easily resolved, and he does so with a characteristic grace and style that are difficult to resist. In a sense, Fergusson is indeed a Western writer; but he is most certainly not a writer of "Westerns"—an unfortunate confusion on which many of the area's serious literary artists have been cruelly impaled.

As a Westerner (and more specifically a Southwesterner) Fergusson, as Cecil Robinson points out, "has satisfied Allen Tate's prime requisite for the authentic regional writer: he is a native."[1] "Regional writer," it seems to me, is a tag that should imply neither praise nor blame; it is usually a circumstance of nativity and upbringing over which an author has no control. But Fergusson, like most of his Western colleagues, has been victimized by both devotees and detractors of that nebulous concept. In the 1920's and 1930's, when a great many people were bravely asserting that "regionalism" was *the* key to a proper understanding of American literature and culture, he was often cited as a promising young Southwesterner who might some day help justify the theory of literary regionalism. In the 1950's and 1960's, when the term "regionalist" became a favorite pejorative of critics and reviewers, Fergusson—who long since had been branded as a provincial writer—shared in the abuse heaped on the regionalist as a generical type. Both responses to the author, I believe, are inaccurate, for Fergusson's novels, as Lawrence Clark Powell has observed, are "at the pinnacle of Southwestern fiction, true to life and love and landscape."[2] In the author's works, landscape is unquestionably important; but in his esthetic priorities, as in those of all good writers, the scene or setting follows life and love.

Fergusson, during his long career, was always something of a maverick, an individualist who declined to conform to the roles others attempted to impose upon him. He was in many ways a rather disturbing and controversial writer—one who developed a full-blown theory of human and social behavior, into which he attempted to fit most of his fictional characters. While I respected and admired the author as craftsman and stylist, I had from the beginning—and still have—reservations concerning certain aspects of his theory; and I freely indicate in this study those areas about which we disagree. In this regard, I concede that I possess no elevated perch from which to pronounce infallible judgment; I can only draw on personal experience and observation; and it is entirely possible that the author was wholly right and I wrong. I hope, in any case, that, in stating Fergusson's position, I have in no way distorted his beliefs; but I admit that, in summarizing anything, there is inevitably a loss of continuity and fullness. Therefore, the best course of action open to anyone truly interested in Fergusson—and one that I heartily recommend—is that such a person read the works and then judge for himself the validity of the writer's premises and assumptions. Indeed, I shall be satisfied if this book serves merely to suggest areas of controversy relative to Fergusson's concepts upon which a reader may focus his intellectual energies.

My approach in the ensuing pages is to establish, following the usual biographical sketch, the main points of the author's philosophy and to use as primary sources for this task his books *Modern Man* and *People and Power*. From that vantage point I have surveyed the remaining works, more or less in the order in which they were published. The final chapter, which offers a summary of Fergusson's theories concerning literature and writing, is also a brief attempt to measure the dimensions of his accomplishment. Though I make numerous comments about his style and his methods of characterization and plotting, I have not intended this book to be a close analysis of the various technical aspects of the writer's works. Many topics concerning Fergusson

Preface

and his writing remain to be explored; and my investigation here, I admit, develops only a few of these topics.

Harvey Fergusson died in August, 1971. Before his death Mr. Fergusson offered, through correspondence, suggestions for the planning and early preparation of this study. In 1968, I personally interviewed the writer in Berkeley, California, his home during the last three decades of his life. He answered questions concerning his biography and his books, and he generously allowed me to examine his papers and manuscripts in the Bancroft Library of the University of California at Berkeley. The most interesting feature of those papers is the author's journal, which covers more than half a century. I have not quoted from the journal since its contents are, for the most part, of a personal nature; but reading it provided valuable background and perspective from which to evaluate the writer's published works.

For assistance of various kinds I want to express my sincere appreciation to the following people: Mr. Saul Cohen of Santa Fe, New Mexico; Miss Quail Hawkins of Berkeley; Mrs. Ruby Barker of Stephenville, Texas, who typed the manuscript; Miss Patricia Howard, Acquisitions Librarian of the Bancroft Library; librarians of the Mary Couts Burnett Library of Texas Christian University; and, most important of all, my wife Betsy, to whom the book is dedicated.

Before his death Harvey Fergusson kindly granted me permission to quote from his works. In addition, grateful acknowledgement is made to William Morrow and Company, which owns copyright to the following books: _The Blood of the Conquerors, Capitol Hill, Women and Wives, Hot Saturday, Wolf Song, In Those Days, Footloose McGarnigal, Rio Grande, Modern Man, The Life of Riley, People and Power, Grant of Kingdom,_ and _The Conquest of Don Pedro._ Quotations from these works are used by permission of William Morrow and Company, Inc. Hawthorn Books owns copyright to _Home in the West,_ and quotations from that work are used by permission of Hawthorn Books, Inc.

WILLIAM T. PILKINGTON

Tarleton State University
Stephenville, Texas

Chronology

1890	Harvey Fergusson born January 28 in Albuquerque, New Mexico, the second of Harvey Butler and Clara Huning Fergusson's four children.
1899	Was given his first horse and gun; began his wanderings as a solitary hunter across northern New Mexico.
1906	Began an academic year at the New Mexico Military Institute in Roswell.
1907	Enrolled in Washington and Lee University at Lexington, Virginia.
1911	Received Bachelor of Arts degree from Washington and Lee University; returned to New Mexico and became a ranger in the Forest Service, working in the Kit Carson National Forest.
1912	Went to Washington, D. C., at his father's urging; obtained a job as reporter for the Washington *Herald;* later worked for several other newspapers.
1913	Sold his first short story to a pulp magazine, *The Black Cat.*
1915	Spent the first of many summers in New Mexico; took a job with Frederic J. Haskin, who wrote a syndicated newspaper column; as Haskin's assistant for several years, traveled throughout United States, Canada, and Latin America.
1917	Met H. L. Mencken.
1919	Began writing his first novel, working during his spare time.
1921	*The Blood of the Conquerors.*
1923	*Capitol Hill;* moved to New York City and became

	a free-lance writer; sold fiction to various mass-circulation magazines.
1924	*Women and Wives.*
1926	*Hot Saturday.*
1927	*Wolf Song;* lived briefly in Salt Lake City; married Rebecca McCann, who died of pneumonia later the same year; returned to New York.
1929	*In Those Days.*
1930	*Footloose McGarnigal.*
1931	Moved to Hollywood and began ten-year career as part-time scriptwriter for several motion picture companies.
1933	*Rio Grande.*
1936	*Modern Man.*
1937	*The Life of Riley.*
1942	Terminated his association with the movie industry; moved his residence permanently to Berkeley, California.
1944	*Home in the West.*
1947	*People and Power.*
1950	*Grant of Kingdom.*
1954	*The Conquest of Don Pedro,* a Literary Guild selection.
1971	August 27, died at his home in Berkeley.

CHAPTER 1

The Writer and His Country

ALBUQUERQUE, New Mexico, a quintessentially Southwestern city, is arid in climate, almost a mile high in altitude, and is lighted by a brassy sun that, at midday, seems welded to a bright, blue sky. East of town, the magnificent Sandia Mountains rise to meet a purple haze; to the north, west, and south, wastelands of desert and rock stretch as far as the imagination is able to follow them. In an arid land, rivers are the first necessity for the growth of any human society, and flowing through the center of Albuquerque is the storied Rio Grande, the community's artery of life; and irrigated farms—as well as mesquite, cottonwood trees, and assorted weeds along the river's banks—form a ribbon of green in an otherwise brown and barren landscape. Albuquerque, as Lawrence Clark Powell has truly said, is at "the heart of the Southwest . . . the *cor cordium*."[1]

But quite apart from its regional peculiarities, which unquestionably lend the city much of its charm and beauty, Albuquerque (unlike its neighbor Santa Fe, eighty miles to the north) is also quintessentially American. In its historical development, its recent rapid growth, its racial conflicts, and its stratified social structure, it fits into an urban pattern than many Americans from other areas easily recognize because they were reared in a similar environment. Over the past century, every advancement in transportation—railroad, automobile, airplane—has given new impetus to Albuquerque's rapid expansion in both land and population. From a small ingrown town of twenty thousand at the turn of the century to an urban complex of more than a quarter million in the 1970's, it has become a financial, trading, and educational center for an entire region—a "city" in every sense of the

15

word, with all the advantages and problems that the term implies.

Harvey Fergusson was born in Albuquerque in 1890, and he was manifestly a product of its special ambience. Though he did not reside there after 1912, he returned to his birthplace many times over the years; and, despite attempts to escape the town and everything it represents, the man—and, of course, his works as an extension of the man—was marked irrevocably by New Mexico in general and by Albuquerque in particular. And, just as Albuquerque's history is prototypical of that of dozens of American cities, Fergusson's career—beginning around the turn of the century and ending with the author's death in August, 1971—is a case study which well illustrates the experiences of many twentieth-century American writers. Fergusson had an excellent opportunity to observe, from varying angles and over an extended period, changes in the country's literature and society; and change—both personal and social—is one of the recurring subjects of his fiction. Hopefully, then, a brief recounting of the author's life and a somewhat fuller consideration of his works will be of some value in illuminating America's recent literary and social history.

I *Family Background*

As is true of most people's, Fergusson's biography does not begin with the mere fact of his birth.[2] The forces and people, the ideas and ancestors, that shape an individual extend farther back than he can ever know. One of Fergusson's books, *Home in the West,* is, in part at least, a fascinating autobiographical account of the writer's early years; more precisely it is, as the subtitle indicates, *An Inquiry into My Origins.* The literary and social significance of *Home in the West* is discussed on subsequent pages, but for the present I wish to use the work as a chief source in reconstructing the author's family background and his early experiences. As autobiography, the account ends, however, about 1920, after the writer had acquired his first job as a newspaper reporter in Washington, D. C.

Both sides of Fergusson's family, as he explains in his book, played important roles in New Mexico's nineteenth-century history and development. His maternal grandfather, Franz Huning, was a German farm boy, one of thirteen children, who came to America in 1848. Upon his death half a century later, Huning left an unpublished personal memoir which Fergusson, at the beginning of *Home in the West,* quotes from and summarizes (and uses elsewhere, incidentally, as the basis for some of his fiction, particularly the novel *In Those Days).* As a child, Huning was curious and adventurous; and he came to America with the highest expectations. He went first to St. Louis, where, hoping to move on to California, he got a job driving oxen on freight caravans on the Santa Fe Trail. He saw Santa Fe, at the end of the long trail, for the first time on Christmas Day, 1850, and he remained a New Mexican from that moment to the end of his life.

Santa Fe in 1850, says Fergusson, was "the strangest confluence of human types and energies that ever existed on this continent"[3]—an unlikely assemblage of Mexican aristocrats and peons, Indians of every variety, mountain men, freighters, and United States troopers. Such a place seemed to offer a golden opportunity to an enterprising young man like Franz Huning. He stayed in Santa Fe, worked as a clerk in several mercantile stores, then bought his own small store which promptly failed. The greatest adventure of Huning's life occurred in 1851 when he and some companions trekked into Apache country to buy cheap mules that the Indians had stolen in Mexico. That venture also failed when the expedition was trapped in a snowstorm in the White Mountains of what is now Arizona, and Huning was lucky to escape with his life.

After his unfortunate experiences in Santa Fe, the young German moved to Albuquerque. Again he worked for a while as a clerk, after which his scholarly inclinations secured for him a position as secretary and interpreter for a priest; and he later acquired a similar position with a federal judge. In 1857, he opened a store on the plaza in Albuquerque; and the next twenty-five years, writes his grandson, were "a period of growing prosperity and power. Success caught up with him, piled its burdens on his back, interrupted that long train of thought and dream which had begun in the German forest."[4] The cavalry troops stationed in the area were the making of Huning's enterprise, and the Civil War in particular proved a boon to his store. After he had a little money, he began to expand, building a flour mill and sawmill and buying nearby farms and ranches. He married a Bavarian girl he had met in St. Louis; and in the 1880's, at the height of his power, he built in Albuquerque an enormous house which he modeled after a German castle on the Rhine; indeed, the structure came to be popularly known as "Castle Huning."

According to Fergusson, Franz Huning was not essentially a businessman; in fact, he disliked and distrusted the kind of urban businessman that the railroads brought to town in the late nineteenth century. Huning was a merchant-adventurer, a creature of the old Southwest who was wholly alien to the bustling commercial atmosphere of turn-of-the-century Albuquerque. Huning consciously passed up a chance to become a financial giant, a millionaire; and in his old age his possessions had dwindled to his beloved castle and the land on which it stood.

As a boy, Fergusson says, he never really knew his grandfather, though he often wandered through the castle or explored its grounds. Only when he read the old man's personal reminiscences many years later did the writer begin to understand his grandfather and discover in him a kindred spirit—almost, it seems, an alter ego. Many facets of Huning's character—his curiosity, his desire for adventure, his love of books and learning, his impatience with the mechanics of moneymaking—Fergusson believes were inherited by himself. "I felt," he writes after having read his grandfather's memoir, "as though I had then discovered the source of many of my most persistent traits and impulses."[5]

Fergusson's paternal grandfather was a Southern aristocrat, Sampson Noland Ferguson (the extra s was added to the family name, for unknown reasons, by the writer's father); and, before the Civil War, he owned a large cotton plantation in Pickens County, Alabama. About this grandfather the author knows little except that he was ruined by the Civil War and had nothing to bequeath his son, Harvey Butler Fergusson, except a name, a heritage, and at least the beginnings of an education. He sent his son to Washington College in Lexington, Virginia, which at the time was presided over by General Robert E. Lee. Harvey Butler Fergusson, the writer's father, stayed for seven years at Washington College where he acquired both a liberal arts education and a law degree. After joining a law firm in Wheeling, West Virginia, he was sent in 1881 to White Oaks, New Mexico, to protect a client's mining claim there. In White Oaks, he roomed with three remarkable young men—William MacDonald, who was to become a governor of New Mexico; Albert B. Fall, Secretary of the Interior during President Warren G. Harding's administration and a central figure in a celebrated scandal; and Emerson Hough, later a popular and best-selling novelist. (White Oaks, as a matter of fact, is the setting of Hough's novel *Heart's Desire: The Story of a Contented Town;* and Fergusson's father supposedly became one of the tale's minor characters.)

From the beginning, the elder Fergusson was attracted to the go-for-broke society he found in the newly opened West. In 1883, deciding that Albuquerque was New Mexico's city of the future, he moved there; and he discovered almost immediately that he had at least two talents that were useful in such a place—"a gift for dramatizing himself and a gift of eloquent speech."[6] In Albuquerque, the young lawyer's practice soon flourished. He entered politics—as an unreconstructed Southern Democrat—and was quickly acclaimed a great orator. In large part because of the state's "east side," settled principally by ranchers and dryland farmers from Texas and Oklahoma, his political career advanced rapidly. He was first elected a territorial delegate to Washington; then, after New Mexico achieved statehood, he was twice sent to the national House of Representatives. He seems to have been a kind of aristocratic Populist since he loudly approved, on more than one occasion, the "rising tide of indignation against government of the special interests, by the special interests, and for the special interests."[7] The common people, both Anglo and Spanish, usually supported his candidacy—as well, of course, as New Mexico's large contingent of transplanted Southerners. Though, according to his son, he "showed astonishing spizzerinctum"[8] as a politician, the elder Fergusson never attained his cherished goal of becoming a United States senator.

Somewhat incongruously, the ambitious politician became a friend of the aging merchant-adventurer; and in the 1880's he married Franz Huning's daughter Clara. As a wedding gift, Franz gave the couple an adobe house in Old Town, not far from "Castle Huning," which became the family home (and the adobe house remains to this day an Albuquerque landmark[9]). Fergusson's admiration for his father appears to have been considerably more restrained than that which he felt for his maternal grandfather. "I liked my father," he says; "I admired him with some reservations. . . ."[10] The reservations had mostly to do with his father's being wedded, on the one hand, too closely to the past—to the Southerner's bittersweet love of tragedy and defeat. On the other hand, as a Westerner, the elder Fergusson professed to believe "passionately in ambition, fortune, personal triumph, and that belief was the religion of the world in which he lived and worked."[11] He seems to have taken as his own the worst elements of two traditions, and for that his son could never quite forgive him.

II   Growing Up in Albuquerque

Harvey Fergusson was the second of Harvey Butler and Clara Huning Fergusson's four children. The eldest was Erna, who became a successful writer of travel books and an indefatigable literary promoter of the Southwest; her *Our Southwest* (1940), incidentally, is still, for the casual reader, the best general introduction to the region. The youngest child, Francis, is now a well-known scholar, writer, and professor of literature; his most widely read book is probably *The Idea of a Theater* (1949), and he has done in addition significant scholarly work on Classical literature and on Dante. Even the third child, Lina, seems to have been bitten by the family literary bug; for she has recently edited a selection of J. Ross Browne's letters and journals.[12]

Harvey, born in 1890, was from the beginning a solitary child, not given to close friendships.[13] In school he was, by his own admission, far from being a noted scholar, and he was shy and awkward in any kind of social situation. Having been hit in the eye with a batted ball at age eight, he quickly developed an aversion to organized sports. Rather than cultivate a circle of playmates or any athletic ability he might have possessed, he formed instead an affection for horses and the outdoors. His father encouraged him while he was still quite young to roam the fields and marshes near the Rio Grande, to become a solitary hunter and individualist. Over the years the boy widened his explorations and in time became intimately familiar with hundreds of square miles of what was still wilderness area. He also developed a permanent love for hunting and fishing, pastimes that later, when he was a busy man of the world, afforded him much pleasure and recreation.

Artistically, the greatest early influence on Fergusson was that of his mother. She had been educated by tutors and in a convent in St. Louis, and she encouraged her son in all his artistic endeavors. At first, Fergusson's primary interest was seemingly in the graphic arts—sketching and drawing—and his practice in these arts taught him to observe keenly and in detail. Gradually, though, his attention shifted to literature. As a boy, his reading included Rudyard Kipling, Henry David Thoreau, and other comparable writers. By his late teens, however, he had discovered H. L. Mencken, Van Wyck Brooks, Randolph Bourne, and "all the other bright young prophets of a new day."[14] They told him that "the United States was a great physical hulk of a mechanical civilization without culture, charm or individuality. Its morality was primitive, repressive, and hypocritical. Its intellectual life was mostly a lame apology for its greed. Its politics were corrupt, bombastic, and ridiculous. For the fine arts it was a desert where talent either starved to death or was corrupted."[15] These propositions Fergusson had already pretty much arrived at on his own, and the testimony of influential and rhetorically accomplished writers merely confirmed his existing beliefs.

Fergusson's intellectual development in this regard, of course, fits a fairly well-defined pattern: his was an oft-repeated reaction among intelligent young people during the early decades of the twentieth century when most Americans lived in small towns and ethical and social attitudes were pervaded by middle-class values. Certainly the Southwest during those years—like any provincial backwater area—was notably inhospitable to its sensitive, talented young; and many of these young people were forced to abandon their native region in search of more salubrious intellectual climates. In effect, this is what Fergusson had to do. As he describes Albuquerque at the beginning of the twentieth century, it was little more than an overgrown village—isolated, puritanical in its public moral life, rigidly structured socially, and full of "babbitry" and stupidity. As a boy, he escaped the town by means of extended hunting expeditions; as a man, he escaped it by pursuing his destiny in large cities. It was inevitable, therefore, that from an early age he was, at least spiritually, a recruit in Mencken's army of rebels who were then attacking the citadels of small-town and middle-class America.

Fergusson started to write, with some degree of seriousness, at about age fifteen when he began pouring all his rapidly evolving ideas and impressions into a journal. At age sixteen, he was sent to the New Mexico Military Institute at Roswell where many unpleasant experiences created in him a lasting antipathy to regimentation in all its forms, whether military or civilian. At age seventeen, he was enrolled in his father's old school, now called Washington and Lee University, in Lexington, Virginia. Fergusson found that the college had not changed much since his father's day; its reason for existing was still, first and foremost, "to produce Southern gentlemen,"[16] and he was subjected to all the indoctrination and essentially extraneous activities that were required for this purpose. For example, he joined one of the many highly organized fraternities on campus, had some small success as a member, and ended up despising both himself and the fraternity for his acquiescence to the system. He concedes that he was not generally popular among his classmates; he was most of the time either callow and cynical or sullenly brooding about some hopeless love affair in which he was engaged. For a young intellectual such as Fergusson, the best part of college life was his discovery of the library, where for the first time in his experience he began to read widely and seriously. After four years of alternating failure and frustration with (as he believed) only minor compensations, he received his degree and returned with high hopes to New Mexico.

In Albuquerque, he first secured a job as an electrician's assistant, a position for which he had no aptitude. That lasted a week. His next job, in which he found a measure of satisfaction, was as a ranger in the Forest Service, working in the Kit Carson National Forest in northern New Mexico. The work was physically exhausting, a circumstance that proved to have its advantages. Looking back on the experience, Fergusson writes: "There is a kind of reassurance in the discovery that life can be reduced to such simple terms, that energy can be burned to the last ounce, that hunger can be an all-absorbing passion and sleep sweeter than any luxury."[17] During his few periods of leisure, he amused himself by writing stories, none of which he felt was worthy of being submitted for publication.

At this point in 1912, after he had worked for two summer seasons as a forest ranger, Fergusson's father intervened in his life for what turned out to be the last and most critical time. He told his son to come to Washington, where he was serving one of his two terms in the House of Representatives as congressman from New Mexico. The congressman had secured a job for his son—a sinecure really—in the folding room of the House Office Building, folding speeches to be mailed by representatives to their constituents. He also planned for the younger Fergusson to work toward a law degree by attending night classes at a local law school.

Fergusson agreed to his father's proposal and left Albuquerque for good. When he left, he departed with a sense of relief and with the hope that he might find a gentler, more tolerant society in which to live and work. Over the years his attitudes toward his birthplace mellowed and became more philosophical, and he returned to Albuquerque many times for visits of varying duration. But he never again made New Mexico his official residence.

It is interesting, in this regard, to follow the author's comments about Albuquerque during the course of his long career. In the 1920's, for instance, a decade and more after his departure, he was still an angry rebel. In an interview in 1926, he told a newspaper reporter, obviously referring to the town where he grew to manhood: "The artist during this century and part of the last has been a pariah in his community. In the nature of modern civilization he cannot be a functional part of this scene. An intellectual simply can't live in a small American town."[18] By the early 1940's, however, when he was writing *Home in the West*, he had acquired a more detached and balanced perspective: the town, he had come to realize, though often cruel and insensitive, was simply a victim of "the immaturity common to all rapidly growing organisms. It was not interested in individual development, it was interested in social progress."[19]

In 1955, Fergusson was asked to revisit Albuquerque, after a prolonged absence, in order to write a preface for a new edition of one of his books. He was astonished by the town's tremendous growth since he had last seen it—growth not only in buildings and people but in "the variety and freedom of human association which always seemed to me one of the great values of major cities." He concluded that "If I were young and had strong legs, it would please me now to live once more in my native town."[20]

III   *Life as a Writer*

After Fergusson left Albuquerque in 1912, to join his father in
Washington, he began law classes and worked at a new job. He
soon discovered the Library of Congress, which, because of his
father's official position, he was allowed to use much as he
pleased. Though he was by this time thoroughly disenchanted
with his home town, he remembered the West's history and its
open country with nothing but affection. Out of nostalgia, he
began to read extensively in the Library's collection of Western
Americana, an activity that served him well in his later writing
career. Fergusson also began to feel after a few weeks in
Washington that his destiny lay not in a law office but in some
form of literary pursuit. Like so many American writers of the
late nineteenth and early twentieth centuries, his entry to a writing career, as it turned out, was through newspapers and journalism.

Quickly bored with his job in the House Office Building, he
began hanging around the offices of the old *Washington Herald,*
which was then one of the worst of Washington's many bad
newspapers. Though he received no remuneration, he covered a
number of minor events for the *Herald,* writing brief accounts of
them. Finally, one of his dispatches caught the eye of an editor,
and he was offered a paying job at eight dollars a week. "I have
never forgotten the feeling of lightness and hope," an older Fergusson remembers in *Home in the West,* "the singing joy of that
first success. At last I had found something I could do and
wanted to do and could earn my bread by doing. For the first
time in my life, I truly believe, I felt wholly at one with the social world—felt as though my tiny trickle of energy was flowing
spontaneously into the great total stream of human effort."[21]

The same day the newspaper job was offered him, he withdrew
from law school, sold his textbooks for sixteen dollars, and began
his career as a journalist. Within a few months he had obtained a
better-paying job on the *Morning News* in Savannah, Georgia,
where he stayed for about six months. After a brief tenure with
the *Richmond Times-Dispatch,* he found a position on the
Washington bureau of the *Chicago Record-Herald* where he
helped cover the Illinois state delegation to Congress.

About 1915, Fergusson made the first of his many return visits to New Mexico. He spent the summer and all of his money wandering around the countryside with a friend, reliving boyhood experiences. Summer visits to the West—to high, dry Rocky Mountain country—were to punctuate the writer's life for years to come. As he reports in *Home in the West*, from October to April he could be fairly content as a city-dweller. The sights, sounds, and smells of spring, however, always roused in him a desire for wide open spaces: "I became sick for space, altitude, and a view without a house."[22] Indeed, this desire for more personal freedom—in particular, the freedom to commute between winters in the East and summers in New Mexico—prompted him to turn seriously to the writing of fiction.

One of the crucial events of Fergusson's early career occurred at the end of that first vacation in New Mexico. Returning to Washington penniless, he took the first job offered him—as assistant to the creator of the Frederic J. Haskin "Newsletter," a popular syndicated newspaper column. From the start, Haskin more or less turned the writing of the feature over to Fergusson, who composed more than one thousand five hundred "letters" under Haskin's name. A valuable byproduct of his work with Haskin was that for several years Fergusson, in search of material, was allowed to travel extensively across the United States, Canada, and Latin America.

Perhaps the most significant occurrence during that time, however, was Fergusson's meeting H. L. Mencken. Mencken was a friend of Haskin's; and, in 1917 through the latter's agency, Fergusson was granted an interview with the great man. When Fergusson, following the interview, wrote a laudatory piece about Mencken's works in progress, their acquaintance began to flourish. At the time Mencken was the leader and principal inspiration of a group of young iconoclasts—writers and intellectuals, many of whom were themselves decamped regionals, whose chief goal was the destruction of middle-class values in general and small-town fundamentalist rigidity in particular. Much of their work appeared in the *Smart Set* magazine and later in Mencken's *American Mercury*. Invariably Mencken's relationship with such people was as mentor to pupil, and Fergusson realized from the beginning that his friendship with such a famous man must, of necessity, be structured somewhat along those lines. Mencken seemed to be looking for an intellectual heir whom he could indoctrinate and mold into an imitation of the master, and Fergusson consciously played the role of innocent disciple; in private he scarcely ever agreed—at least not completely—with Mencken's fulminations and tirades on various subjects. Fergusson, using his privileges in the Library of Congress, continued to read widely—everything from great novelists such as Leo Tolstoy, Gustave Flaubert, and Thomas Hardy to the works of contemporary psychoanalysts. As a result, his interests and beliefs began to transcend the sometimes narrow concerns of his older friend.

But the young writer's relationship with Mencken was not without compensations. For one thing, Mencken was a prodigious and entertaining talker; and, even when Fergusson did not agree with what he heard, listening was usually an enjoyable experience. More to the point—and a primary reason for the friendship, of course—was the fact that Mencken proved to be of inestimable value in advancing Fergusson's career. From the first, Mencken encouraged the younger man to write fiction, to give up his newspaper work, and to devote full time to more creative projects. This Fergusson finally did in 1923 when he moved from Washington to New York and became a free-lance writer.

Mencken's advice in this regard was a reliable and steadying influence. Today Fergusson's journalism, the result of a decade's work, is scattered about in minor newspapers, and much of it is irrecoverable; to speak bluntly, it is of little or no interest to the student of literature. The years spent as a journalist, however, were not wasted; they were a useful apprenticeship. The nature of many of his assignments as a newspaperman engendered in him a lifelong interest in man's social and political life, which, in one way or another, is the subject of almost all his fiction. His experiences as a reporter, moreover, trained him to be a clear-headed and interested observer—training that is admirably reflected in his later writings. And, most important of all, writing for newspapers disciplined his style, which became one of the more attractive features of his later works. In *Home in the West*, Fergusson confesses that, when he first began to write, he imitated his father's rather flowery speaking manner: "I composed long, oratorical sentences, perfect in sound and small in sense. All my progress was a struggle for simplicity and precision."[23] Since his newspaper work helped teach him the value of word economy, it was the first step in that struggle.

Fergusson's career as a publishing fiction writer had actually begun in 1913 when he had sold a story to a magazine called *The Black Cat*. Throughout his years as a journalist, he continued to write and sell fiction. At first, declining to use his best and most original ideas, he wrote only formula stories aimed strictly at the pulp magazine market. Then, in 1919, he began to work on a story that truly held his interest—a novel set in modern-day New Mexico. Working on weekends and during vacations, he finished the book in a year and a half; then he took the manuscript to Mencken who was a member of the board of directors of the Alfred A. Knopf publishing company. Mencken liked the work, and Knopf published it in 1921 under the title *The Blood of the Conquerors*. From that date on, Fergusson was widely recognized as a well-established writer.

Throughout the 1920's, his friend Mencken saw to it that his novels were published and that their dust covers were adorned with enthusiastic blurbs. *Capitol Hill* and *Women and Wives*, stories set primarily in Washington, appeared in 1923 and 1924. In 1926, *Hot Saturday*, a tale of the contemporary Southwest, was published. The first of the writer's great novels based on Southwestern history, *Wolf Song* and *In Those Days*, were brought out in 1927 and 1929. And the appearance in 1930 of *Footloose McGarnigal*, another of his fictional studies of the modern Southwest, capped a remarkably productive decade. Mencken during those years also persuaded Charles C. Baldwin to include Fergusson in the latter's influential *The Men Who Make Our Novels*. "When I asked Mr. Mencken," Baldwin begins, "to nominate someone or other for inclusion in my book, he named Harvey Fergusson as the best of the new men."[24]

But, despite the generally favorable critical reception of his books and the praise heaped upon them by Mencken and others, Fergusson found it necessary, after his removal to New York, to make the preponderance of his livelihood by doing things other than serious fiction-writing. For a while he worked for a public-relations firm; but he gradually discovered that he could make a great deal of money with very little effort by doing hack work for various mass-circulation magazines. In particular, because they had once worked for Knopf, he knew the editors at *McCall's* and *Redbook*, and he sold numerous stories to these women's magazines, averaging for several years about one thousand dollars a month on the sale of his shorter pieces. Fergusson was not proud of these stories, but he found them—as did F. Scott Fitzgerald at about the same time—a necessary expedient for making money. He called them "potboilers," and he discouraged potential readers from attempting to exhume them from the obscurity in which they rested. He believed, in fact, that the only one of his periodical stories from the 1920's with any genuine literary merit was "The New Englander," published in the February, 1926, issue of *The American Mercury*.

In January, 1927, Fergusson married Rebecca McCann. (In 1919, the author was briefly and unhappily married to a girl named Polly Pretty, a marriage he satirizes in the novel *Women and Wives*.) Rebecca McCann wrote and illustrated an inspirational syndicated newspaper feature called "The Cheerful Cherub." After their marriage, the couple moved to Salt Lake City. In Mary Graham Bonner's introduction to a collection called *The Complete Cheerful Cherub*, an account of Rebecca and Harvey Fergusson's marriage is provided: "Here [in Salt Lake City] they climbed mountains, worked and mapped out their future . . . they were supremely congenial and happy. They left here in December. They were going to spend Christmas with Harvey's family in Albuquerque. . . . He drove the car down in a snowstorm, feeling it unwise for her to take such an arduous trip. . . . She met Harvey in Albuquerque. But a slight cold turned into a heavy one. . . . She was ill only a few days. . . ."[25] The dedication of *Wolf Song*, published during the year of their marriage, reads, "For Rebecca." Following Rebecca's death from pneumonia at the end of 1927, the writer never remarried.

After his brief residence in Salt Lake City, Fergusson returned for several years to New York. He went to California for the first time in 1931 when a Hollywood agent read his novels and became convinced that he had great potential as a screen writer. Once in California, the author quickly found a job at Paramount Studios. For years Fergusson was advised by friends and colleagues that "Hollywood will get you yet."[26] But it never did.·He used it as a kind of meal ticket, working there six months of the year and employing the other six months for travel and serious writing. For ten years he maintained this arrangement, and he completed three full-length works during that period. One of these, *Rio Grande* (1933), a marvelously readable history of New

Mexico's great river valley, is among his three or four best books. The other two, *Modern Man: His Belief and Behavior* (1936) and *The Life of Riley* (1937), are revealing and generally interesting, but they certainly cannot be placed in the front rank of the author's works. As a screen writer, Fergusson worked for several companies during his decade in Hollywood. He was involved in a number of team-writing projects, and he seems to have specialized in movie "treatments." (A "treatment" is a narrative summary of a movie's plot written before the composition of an actual script.) The only script that Fergusson was wholly responsible for writing was for an eminently forgettable opus called *Stand Up and Fight,* based on the life of Daniel Boone.

IV *The Berkeley Years*

Fergusson first went to Berkeley, California, for extended stays during the 1930's, though at the time, of course, his primary responsibility was in Los Angeles. He went to Berkeley because his sister Lina lived there and because it was geographically closer to both Hollywood and New Mexico than was New York. Beginning in 1931, he had made his official residence in Los Angeles for several years; but he soon decided that he did not wish to live in that extraordinary place any longer than was absolutely necessary. So he moved to Berkeley for good in 1942, living for many years just off the campus of the University of California. In the 1940's, his writing interests turned from fiction to subjects of more immediate concern during those war and post-war years—subjects mostly social and political in nature. *Home in the West,* published in 1944, is partially an autobiography; but it is also, as has been indicated already, a social document of no small significance. Using the facilities of the University of California library, he wrote during the decade *People and Power: A Study of Political Behavior in America* (1947), an argument, rooted in extensive reading and research, for post-war economic development.

Late in the 1940's, Fergusson's passion for fiction seems to have been eagerly renewed; and he once again began working on a novel. His final published books, in fact, are novels; and they represent the crowning achievement of a long and distinguished career. *Grant of Kingdom* (1950) and *The Conquest of Don Pedro* (1954) are discussed in detail later; for the moment it must be sufficient to note that they have been widely acknowledged as major contributions to Western American literature—indeed, many believe they are major contributions to American literature generally. During the nearly two decades that elapsed between publication of *The Conquest of Don Pedro* and the author's death, Fergusson continued to write. He began a number of projects and completed at least one other novel. He shelved the finished manuscript, however, without even attempting to get it published because, as he believed, "it is too alien to contemporary literary fashion for writing about misery, violence, and perversion, the unholy trinity of publishing success."[27]

Though physically hampered by arthritis and advancing age, Fergusson retained to the end an alert mind and a fierce drive to create lasting literature. "If I couldn't write," he said not long before his death, "I don't think I could live."[28] During his last years, Fergusson occupied a small apartment in the lovely Berkeley hills behind the University of California campus. He died of a massive heart attack on August 27, 1971.

CHAPTER 2

Modern Man and His Society

CONCERNING Fergusson's fourteen published books, one general characteristic is immediately evident: the broader the canvas, the less satisfactory the work. This rule of thumb, I believe, applies to a great many writers whose primary gift is in the area of narrative and fiction-writing. When such a writer tries to cover too much ground—when, in particular, he yields to the temptation to find the answer, the big solution, to some vexing, complicated problem—he seems doomed from the start. His argument, whatever its merits, is lost on many readers who are quickly distracted by their private sport of finding exceptions to sweeping generalizations, and who in fact often become intent on undermining the author's entire line of reasoning. Paradoxically, when the writer restricts his work to following a few people through a series of closely related situations in a carefully controlled landscape, he is usually more successful in both a general and a specific sense: the reader, caught up in an absorbing narrative, is ordinarily much readier to grant that the story's people, events, and resolutions of conflict are suggestive, perhaps even universal in their implications, than he would be were he confronted by a contentious treatise on the same subject. Rhetorically, then, such a writer as the one I have described is much more persuasive on the small scale than the large.

Fergusson wrote both "large-scale" and "small-scale" books. As we know, he lived for many years in Washington, the center of the nation's political life; and, as a newspaper reporter for more than a decade, he became fascinated with and was influenced by many opinions about man as a social and political "or-

ganism" (a term he sometimes uses). Many of these observations
and opinions are incorporated in his fiction; and, as elements in
the lives of individual characters, they are provocative and often
convincing. But the author also chose to employ them as the
basis for two works of nonfiction, *Modern Man: His Belief and
Behavior* (1936) and *People and Power: A Study of Political Behavior in America* (1947)—books in which Fergusson generalizes
his experience into a sweeping social and political philosophy.

Modern Man, the first of these works, is concerned principally
with exploring the twentieth-century individual and that
individual's relation to other people and groups. In *People and
Power*, a kind of sequel to *Modern Man*, the focus shifts to society as a whole; and the individual is spotlighted only when the
social unit has some impact upon him. The two books are very
closely related—indeed, they spring from the same premises and
assumptions—and must be considered together. Both books are
weak for basically the same reasons: in general, for the reason already discussed and, in particular, for reasons to be detailed.
But, for the student of Fergusson's fiction, they are interesting
and illuminating reading; and their bearing on the writer's fictional concerns and themes quickly becomes obvious.

I *Modern Man Defined*

Modern Man, published in 1936, is a difficult book to
categorize. Though classified by libraries as a work of philosophy,
the book, Fergusson claimed, was not intended to be purely
philosophical speculation. And indeed much of its content is a
blend of several disciplines of thought and study. The work grew
from the writer's reflections upon himself and his experiences;
and he rather modestly asks "for a tolerant hearing rather than a
complete assent." The book, he continues, "appeals primarily to
shared experience and observation. I believe the reader who has
lived in the same world I have known will find food for his own
thought, and that is all I aspire to offer him."[1] In the course of
his argument, Fergusson supports ideas and generalizations
drawn from personal experience, with frequent allusions to other
works and with a long list of references.

One of the more thought-provoking aspects of *Modern Man* is
what amounts to a theory of mankind's history and development

as a social animal. Fergusson divides this history into three periods: that of primitive man; that of Medieval, or Christian, man; and that of modern man. Twentieth-century America and Western Europe are, of course, comprised mainly of "modern men" (actually Fergusson probably should have called his book *Modern Western Man*, since the title really refers to him). At the moment, however, in various other parts of the world, a good deal of overlapping of the three stages of development exists. In fact, the scheme, though much oversimplified, is a particularly fruitful way of approaching the Southwest, probably the only region in the United States that still has in its population significant numbers of each kind of man.

Fergusson's theories concerning primitive man derive largely from a reading of Sir James George Frazer's *The Golden Bough* and of Franz Boaz's *The Mind of Primitive Man*. Primitive man, the author believes, lives in a simple society, ordinarily one that is highly dependent on the exigencies of nature. Almost all of primitive man's behavior is dictated by the social unit, the group or tribe to which he belongs; and, when the group cannot impose its will by sheer force, it invokes the magical properties of taboo and ritual. Primitive societies, Fergusson asserts, attempt to control their future by making it conform to the past; and in them scarcely any conflict occurs between the individual and society since the concept of an individual consciousness is almost unknown.

Medieval man, according to the author, is the bridge between primitive and modern man. Medieval man is, in every area of his life, Christian—that is, in a historical sense, a functioning part of the Catholic Church. "In theory," writes Fergusson, "Christianity was primitive and absolute, but in its practical workings it was relativistic, and this, to my mind, is what gave it its whole value as a working belief and a means of adaptation" (49). The church found a partial resolution of the growing conflict between individual desires and group pressures in the cycle of sin and confession, for in that cycle men were permitted at least some release for their "sinful" impulses. Medieval Christianity was admittedly rigid and often absolutist, and thinkers were sometimes put to death for their ideas; but at least a measure of implicit recognition of the individual's needs existed within it, and such a recognition was the first step in man's long progress from the primitive stage. The Protestant Reformation, says the author, was an attempt to carry this recognition a step farther, but it proved "a futile compromise. It rejected the rich emotional experience of Catholicism without putting anything in its place" (52).

Modern man, claims Fergusson, is the glorious culmination of a lengthy historical process. Modern man is, above all else, an *individual;* and modern society, the writer argues, provides the best opportunity in human history for the optimum in individual freedom and spontaneity. Although modern man has a possibility for growth and fulfillment that no earlier men possessed, there are still many things about himself, Fergusson believes, that present-day man has not yet learned; therefore, modern man has a way to go before he is ready to exploit the full potential of his situation. Specifically, Fergusson contends that a precondition to modern man's achieving his potential is that he relinquish his "folk belief" in absolute free will—in "The Illusion of Choice" (the title of the book's first section). The notion of free will, he asserts, is the source of such damaging emotions as guilt, remorse, and indignation which are in turn the causes of "disintegration of consciousness which takes a great variety of forms, including almost complete stagnation, neurosis, insanity, and suicide . . ." (15).

Fergusson's ideas, as summarized in *Modern Man,* do not fit neatly into any of the determinist philosophies that have enjoyed some currency in twentieth-century Western thought: strictly speaking, he is not a naturalist, nor is he an oriental fatalist or a psychological behaviorist. Certainly, however, he is convinced that there are definite limitations upon the capacity of an individual to control consciously his destiny. Fairly early in the book the author summarizes his argument as follows:

The scope of my theme may be briefly defined in the form of a few propositions: that man has always had some belief as to the determinants of his behavior; that this belief has always and necessarily involved some measure of illusion; that this illusion, like any other vital illusion, has been a product of the conditions of human life and has borne a necessary relation to them; that the illusion has changed with changing conditions but has always shown a tendency to lag behind them; that during the modern period change has been so rapid and so overwhelming that the illusion [of free will] has fallen into radical disharmony both with the conditions of life, on the one hand, and the state of knowledge on the other, producing a distintegration of consciousness in the most literal sense of the word; and that this disharmony will be gradually ameliorated by the creation of a new illusion, more in harmony with the conditions of modern life and the state of modern knowledge. (10–11)

Implied in the foregoing passage, it seems to me, is the assumption that man's best knowledge about his own behavior is still only a kind of metaphor through which he may perceive something, though not all, of the truth. The metaphor which Fergusson chooses to employ in outlining his theory of behavior is that of equilibrium—of objects balanced on a fulcrum (he calls the second part of his book "The Ethic of Balance"). All truly creative energy, he believes, begins with an impulse, the origin of which is a hidden and sometimes suppressed desire. The proper response to an impulse, says Fergusson, is a process. The impulse prompts a fantasy, which in turn gives rise to reflection, or thought; thought then must issue into action, for in the healthy person all thought must find some outlet in action. (The second step of the process, incidentally, the act of reflection, is the basis for Fergusson's belief in the importance of man's rational faculties; in both *Modern Man* and *People and Power*, he several times expresses his supreme confidence in the efficacy of human reason, when it is properly understood and used.)

The difficulty of an individual's trusting his impulses, claims the author, arises from the circumstance that he is rarely guided by a single impulse; at any given time, he is usually the spiritual battleground for an imposing array of conflicting impulses. At this point, Fergusson introduces the metaphor of balance, which he describes in terms of the simple action of walking: "It is apparent that balance is the essential of all action. All balance is a conflict of forces, sustained and endured. To yield to either of the conflicting forces is to lose balance, and when balance is lost action as such ceases, although movement may continue until an obstacle stops it" (187–88). Internal balance is achieved by man's holding his impulses in suspension, never yielding completely to any one, but providing each its proper outlet. This balance of sometimes conflicting impulses the writer calls the individual's "inner necessity."

In addition, for each individual an "outer necessity"—a complex of demands imposed by the group, or social unit, in which he resides—requires that he achieve a second kind of balance. The behavior of primitive man is governed almost wholly by outer necessity, by the traditional and religious code of his society; and such balance as he achieves is supplied by extrinsic support. Modern man is more willing to obey his impulses; but the behavior of most men, Fergusson asserts, is still far too dependent on the moral dictates of society which are reinforced by widespread fear of public censure. The truly modern individual, the writer states, recognizes that society can make only two legitimate demands of him: that he not resort to violence and that he be honest in fulfilling or abiding by his legal and social contracts. At any rate, once the inner and the outer necessity—and the factors which comprise each—have been brought into equilibrium, a man then acts as he must, seemingly by instinct. He may later rationalize his behavior in terms of "will" or "volition," but in reality he has acted as he has because he has had only one practicable alternative. In this sense, the author believes that the concept of free will is little more than a popular superstition.

A term which recurs time and again in Fergusson's fiction and nonfiction is "destiny." Though he never really defines the word, an individual's destiny appears to be the net result of his actions over a lifetime. A man fulfills his destiny, therefore, in the degree that he behaves in the manner described above (that is, maintains his balance in a world of flux); he denies it to the extent that he irrevocably commits himself to some given course of action and attempts to force his behavior to conform to his will. Man's destiny, the author believes, is something to be discovered, rather than shaped or consciously sought. To yield to destiny, once discovered, is to attain the ultimate in human freedom and spontaneity.

The two most formidable obstacles barring modern man from fully achieving his destiny, Fergusson contends, are his recurring desires to return to the past and the often overwhelming pressures of organized society. Concerning the first, the modern individual must realize that in the contemporary world the only constant is rapid change; and in a state of flux, the writer says, all men exhibit regressive behavior—attempt, in one way or another, to revert to a more orderly past. The truly balanced man, though he can never completely suppress this tendency, is able to live with it; he welcomes change because it is challenging and because he is confident it cannot destroy his equilibrium.

In dealing with group pressures, on the other hand, the author believes that the individual, utilizing the mobility afforded by modern technology, should avoid small social units (small towns in particular) since such groups tend to be rigid and inflexible in their codes of behavior. Modern man should make his livelihood by some specialized form of labor, thus freeing himself from the excessive demands imposed upon the Medieval craftsman. He should, above all, seek his destiny in a large city, which in the modern world provides the greatest variety of human contact and opportunity. "The village and the metropolis," writes Fergusson, "stand at the polar extremes of the modern world . . ." (228). The village is primitive, exacting from its citizens a high degree of moral and social conformity. The city is modern, offering its inhabitants a rich diversity of freedom and independence. Many men, the author realizes, do not want to be independent; they desire the external support of family, neighbors, church, and profession, and thus they often live by choice in villages and small towns. But the truly modern individual, he maintains, is likely to reside in a large city because that is the only place where he is able to escape the bonds of social conformity.

In the third, and last, section of the book, "The Growth of Consciousness," Fergusson supplies his prescription for modern man's continued progress. First, modern man must achieve what the author calls "integration of consciousness," a harmonizing of beliefs (that is, "illusions") and behavior. Men often act in one fashion, out of necessity, while clinging to outmoded beliefs which dictate opposite actions; the results of such a disharmony, Fergusson contends, are the poisonous emotions of guilt and remorse. Contemporary belief, then, must be brought into line with contemporary behavior. Second, modern man must cultivate a continuing "growth of consciousness," an expanding awareness of self and environment and of their relationship. As man's knowledge of himself grows, he will more clearly perceive the significance of his impulses. In any conflict between inner and outer necessity, Fergusson concludes,

Inner necessity always is paramount. Impulse is the substance of life, and discipline its form. Constantly the substance is sacrificed to the form. Impulse is the source, not only of all individual growth, but of all the individual's most vital contributions to the collective consciousness. The deepest despair is not of those who have sinned against society, but of those who have sinned against themselves—who have denied the motion and growth of their own beings. That is why, in the long retrospect, we so seldom regret what we have done and invariably regret what we have not dared to do. (323–24)

As should be obvious from the foregoing discussion (and most obvious of all in the excerpt just quoted), Fergusson's ideas lean heavily on nineteenth-century American philosophy—particularly that of Ralph Waldo Emerson. Though he quotes Emerson by name only a couple of times in *Modern Man*, much of Fergusson's argument has an Emersonian ring to it. Like Emerson, Fergusson is a cosmic optimist, who is confident of man's continued growth and progress; indeed, Fergusson is convinced that his optimism and his unqualified love of life are the views that most clearly distinguish him from a majority of twentieth-century writers and intellectuals. He believes also in the primacy of the individual and in the individual's reliance, as much as is possible, on himself.

Moreover, Fergusson's principal source of self-reliance, the "impulse," seems not much different from Emerson's concept of "intuition." Fergusson affirms, as did Emerson, that the surest means of social improvement is for each individual (compounded many times over, of course) to improve himself—to improve and to strengthen, as Fergusson would have it, his inner and outer balance. While Fergusson would probably deny that he believes in anything remotely resembling Emerson's Oversoul, he does accept the proposition that there is in man and in the universe a mysterious, perhaps divine, force which is in part the origin of an individual's impulses. In this regard, he admits to having some sympathy for the theory of "vitalism," as formulated by Samuel Butler and Henri Bergson—the belief that "there is at work in life a spontaneous or creative force which transcends mechanism" (13). Only in Fergusson's praise of urban life and his faith in technology does he appear to depart from (perhaps "extend" would be a more correct term) Emerson's philosophy.[2]

Though much of the criticism leveled at *Modern Man* when it appeared in 1936 was irrelevant or unfair,[3] the book is not, in all honesty, very convincing. From the perspective of the 1970's, Fergusson's optimism—like Emerson's before him—seems rather tattered and worn; and even in the mid-1930's it had to be maintained in the face of considerable evidence to the contrary. As a contribution to philosophy, psychology, sociology, or whatever, his argument is interesting but dilettantish. The taint of amateurism is readily apparent in the author's scholarship, as exhibited in his list of references, since many of the works cited as sources—popular items in their own day no doubt—have long since passed into the realm of forgotten trivia. In this regard, several professional philosophers and psychologists who reviewed the book when it was published leveled damaging charges against it.[4] One reviewer, for example, suggests that Fergusson's argument is intended "to corroborate his observations rather than to test his hypothesis"[5] (that is, the author is "writing to a thesis," a fatal flaw, it would seem, in any work that professes to be systematic, even semi-scientific, in nature).

In short, *Modern Man* is simply a record of one man's thoughts, based mainly on personal experience; as such, it is readable and occasionally illuminating. But the acceptance of its premises and conclusions by a majority of readers—at the present moment, at least—is inconceivable. The lay reader now finds it too often inconsistent with his own experience, and the professional reader discounts it for improper documentation and faulty methodology. Again, however, my purpose in emphasizing the book is to build a necessary philosophical groundwork from which we may more readily understand Fergusson's other works, especially the fiction; from Fergusson's first book to his last, the ideas developed in *Modern Man* are the vantage point from which he views the spectacle of human behavior.

II *Modern Man as the Common Man*

Many of the theories advanced in *Modern Man* are modified and extended in *People and Power: A Study of Political Behavior in America*, published in 1947. The word "behavior" is, of course, prominently displayed in the subtitles of both *Modern Man* and *People and Power*, and the author contends that, though the second book seems to be a treatise of economics and politics, it is really "a study of human behavior."[6] Specifically, it concerns itself with the typical behavior, multiplied by millions, of that abstraction of political oratory, "the common man." Fergusson believes that, despite misuse and overuse of the term, "common man" designates a useful concept—the average individual in his role as a citizen involved in the social machinery. And just as the average individual is often afflicted in his personal life with a paralyzing disharmony of belief and behavior, so does the American body politic, comprised of millions of typical citizens, suffer from a conflict of ingrained assumptions and beliefs from the past against the rapidly changing conditions of a complex industrial society.

For the average American citizen, the author believes, the most disastrous political illusion is probably that of "individual liberty," which gives rise to another illusion, commonly known as "the American dream." The myth of "individual liberty"—particularly as it embodies a belief in free enterprise and the right of all people to compete fairly in an open-market economy—is manifestly an outgrowth of America's peculiar history. The westward movement of the eighteenth and nineteenth centuries, Fergusson asserts, was motivated by two impulses: the desire to acquire real property, especially cheap land; and the need to escape the restrictions of organized society. The period following the Civil War was admittedly a

. . . paradise for the little entrepreneur. Rich black land was free for the taking. Timber belonged to whoever had an axe or a saw mill. You could take gold from the streams with a pan and shovel. Elk and deer were slaughtered by market hunters and shipped by the carload. All along the Mexican border cattle ran wild and unbranded and so did hogs. Cowboys would kill a calf for breakfast. . . . The means of production then were free to every man. The earth and its fruits belonged to who could use them. Private enterprise was then truly both a right and an opportunity accessible to all. So a great tradition was founded. The tradition still lives but the condition has passed forever. It is hypocrisy to pretend that it still exists. (49–50)

Similarly, the wilderness once harbored rugged individualists who were either incapable or unwilling to function as a part of the social organization. Almost from the beginning, then, the idea of freedom was associated in the popular mind with separation and isolation, conditions that in the middle of the twentieth century are virtually nonexistent. Within the borders of the United States in 1947, when Ferguson was writing, no refuge from the strictures of society, he asserts, remained; perhaps indeed there was no true refuge remaining anywhere on the planet.

Individual liberty in the modern world, the writer contends, if it means anything, means "personal autonomy . . . it means that you are free in the degree that you move upon your own impulses rather than in response to forces outside yourself. It is spontaneity as opposed to compulsion" (58). Genuine liberty is the freedom to grow and to develop one's talents in a civilized and tolerant atmosphere, and one is not likely to find such freedom today in a sparsely populated rural area or small town, locales that now supply "the most reliable mass support for conservatism" (45). Instead, the author claims, large cities, the new "frontiers of social change" (40), are where the American common man attains his highest degree of personal liberty.

Probably the most harmful byproduct of the typical American's belief in free enterprise and rugged individualism, the writer continues, is his extreme reluctance to join formal groups and organizations, even when those groups and organizations are manifestly working in his best interests. As a result, the solitary individual is often left at the mercy of large trading and manufacturing associations whose members conspire to fix wages and prices; in fact, the individual, in conflict with almost any organization of whatever size, is virtually powerless, for "all power is organization and all organization is power. For this reason there is no escape from the pressure of organized power in any society which no longer has a frontier to serve as a place of refuge. Everyone in such a society is either a beneficiary or a victim of organized power" (101). In this regard, Fergusson believes that it is imperative that the common man achieve a new integration of belief and behavior: he must recognize that joining organizations of people whose vested interests are the same as his own will not diminish his freedom but increase it. Thus the author introduces the premise that understanding the dynamics of the organization is increasingly important to modern man's continued well-being.

A large portion of *People and Power,* therefore, is devoted to an examination of the principles of organizational behavior, which the writer believes to be very similar to those of individual behavior. In *Modern Man,* he had already laid the groundwork for this theoretical extension by asserting that "nearly every individual phenomenon has its collective equivalent" (144), and the results of this assumption are everywhere apparent in *People and Power.* In *Modern Man,* for instance, the author advances the theory that the individual who achieves internal equilibrium is the one who manages to balance his conflicting impulses and emotions; in *People and Power*, enlarging his theory by extending its collective implications, he contends that the truly balanced society is one in which there is a maximum number and variety of competing groups and organizations and in which each organized group holds its opposite number in check. In such a situation, presumably, any action taken by public or private authority, in order to gain sufficient backing, would have to be demonstrably in the best interests of the largest number of people.

Any society in which there is only *one* monolithic aggregation of power, Fergusson contends, is a society ruled by tyranny. The most unified and free society is the one that, far from trying to eliminate conflict, manages to bring it into balance: "Balance is conflict among forces that are somewhere near equality in strength and have some common ground upon which to compromise. And the more complex the conflict—the more numerous and various the forces involved—the better the hope of a stable equilibrium" (132). Fergusson's ideas concerning the balanced society, incidentally, seem something of an anticipation of John Kenneth Galbraith's celebrated theory of the modern mammoth economy that is held in suspension by the "countervailing powers" of big business, big labor, and big government—a theory which recently has been vigorously attacked by many political scientists.

In any event, the twentieth-century American, in Fergusson's view, must not only overcome his fear of formal organizations, but also learn to accept the benefits of strong leadership. Inevitably, the author claims, an organization of common men will produce a few *uncommon* men, who quickly rise to positions of leadership. The leader, as Fergusson sees him, is very similar to the highly developed individual described in *Modern Man*—the internally balanced person who is able to maintain his equilibrium in the midst of chaos. The *great* leader is one whose drive for power is tempered by devotion to a worthy ideal; and such a man, the author believes, is one of the finest fruits of modern democracy.

Despite the contempt for the masses expressed by Mencken and other early twentieth-century intellectuals, Fergusson is optimistic that common men will eventually perceive the necessity for exerting organized pressure to attain their desired goals and that they will then act accordingly. The typical American, though his general beliefs may be muddled and excessively sentimental, is often capable of thinking clearly and logically, especially when his method of making a living is concerned. The writer is convinced that technology, in addition to expanding man's freedom through increased mobility and leisure, has required the average man to operate ever more complicated machinery and has thereby taught him to exercise his rational faculties in problem-solving. The common man, therefore, applying the light of reason to his personal situation, will soon realize that his prejudice against concerted action is inimical to his own best interests, and he will become more sophisticated in his political and social behavior. He will also recognize that, in order for industry to grow and the economy to expand, he must constantly increase his consumption of "cultural" goods—that is, "all of those goods men use for their pleasure" rather than for their utility (222). The author concludes that, though the short-run economic and political prospects may be dim (he was of course writing about the years immediately following World War II, when it seemed that the dissolution of the war-time economy might result in serious depression), in the longer view "there is surely some reason to have confidence in the astounding creative power of man—in his ability to remake his environment and in doing so to recreate himself" (241).

Though Fergusson in *People and Power* loosely divides society into the forces of conservatism and reaction on the one hand and those of progress on the other—and obviously favors the latter —he rejects the political nostrums of both right and left since each group seeks to impose its will upon the populace and thus upset the delicate balance of the social mechanism. The writer renounces at once the inert resistance of traditional conservatism and the revolutionary solutions espoused by most forms of radicalism. If Fergusson can be classified politically, he seems to be a kind of nineteenth-century liberal who believes in the inevitability of progress on all levels of society. He affirms, as did the nineteenth-century progressive, that the widest possible suffrage and political participation will result in the greatest social amelioration; he believes, furthermore, that modern industrial democracy, rooted, as it is, in a faith in the average citizen's in-

tegrity and potential, is a sensitive and flexible instrument which
can change to meet changing conditions.

In the interlocking arguments of *Modern Man* and *People and
Power*, as we have seen, the writer explains the basis for his optimism concerning twentieth-century Western society and the
mass of individuals who comprise it. Many of the conclusions
drawn in these two books are soundly reasoned and are grounded
in common sense and close observation of the social reality of the
era from which they spring. Such ambitious and broad-gauge
works, however, rarely confine themselves to descriptions of the
present; almost invariably they attempt to make predictions, both
explicit and implicit, concerning the future. In this regard
Modern Man and *People and Power* are no exceptions: they offer
a detailed picture of the ideal society that the author envisions
and clearly expects to become reality. Unfortunately, when we
test Fergusson's forecasts, made during the 1930's and 1940's,
against present-day conditions, it is striking that, on almost every
large issue about which he speculates, the passage of time has
shown the writer to be wrong. Or, more correctly perhaps, from
the perspective of the 1970's he *seems* to be wrong; the relevance
of his ideas to a world only a few decades removed from the one
he was writing about appears almost nil.

Today, for example, when urban areas are literally crumbling at
the feet of their citizens and when most Americans who can af-
ford to do so are fleeing to small towns and to the countryside,
Fergusson's contention that large cities are the settings most con-
ducive to the growth of human freedom seems amusingly naive.
At a time when the collapse of electoral politics and of democratic
institutions generally is at least a possibility, his nineteenth-
century liberal's faith in the supreme efficacy of democracy seems
rather excessive. When Western society's most popular spokes-
men (Marshall McLuhan, for instance) are proclaiming that
twentieth-century men, in order to survive, must return to a
primitive, tribal situation by abdicating the responsibilities of rational consciousness, Fergusson's praise of modern man's powers
of reasoning seems radically misplaced. And, at a time when the
world's inhabitants are being inundated by the assorted refuse of
dozens of consumer-oriented economies and when the concept of
continual growth as the operating principle of a workable
economy (not to mention a viable planet) has been widely re-

jected, his argument for economic expansion on the basis of geometric increases in the production of consumer and "cultural" goods seems positively alarming.

These are but a few of the objections to Fergusson's theories that come readily to mind; others could easily be assembled. The fact is, of course, that the world in which "modern man" of the 1970's lives is very different from that inhabited by "modern man" of the 1930's and 1940's. Consequently, the author, as a prophet of social and political trends, proved to be not very perspicacious. But then, to be fair, few observers in the 1930's and 1940's who attempted to peer into the future were any more accurate. Certainly the perils of prophecy have embarrassed more than one would-be seer. Luckily for Fergusson, therefore, on most occasions he chose to exercise his talents in forms less hazardous than political and social forecast.

CHAPTER 3

Modern Man in Urban America

FERGUSSON, it seems to me, was much more successful as a social historian (even though his "histories" are ordinarily fictional rather than documented studies) than as a social prophet. Six of his ten novels are set in the present—"the present," in this instance, being the time at which they were written—and, if nothing else, these fictions are useful and entertaining portraits of the life of their times, times which in the 1970's seem almost as remote as the nineteenth-century American West, the setting for the author's remaining four novels. Taken together, the six novels form a unique chronicle of twentieth-century American society, the accumulated social observations of an inquisitive and tenacious writer. A consideration of *Capitol Hill* and *Women and Wives*, two of Fergusson's earliest narratives, seems a good point of departure for assessing the author's fictional output. For one thing these two novels are laid, not in the quaint Southwest, but in large Eastern cities, settings easily recognized by most readers. Moreover, their subject is American political and social behavior, and therefore they obviously relate to the theories advanced in *Modern Man* and *People and Power*, which have just been discussed.

I A Novel of Washington Life

The central character of *Capitol Hill*, published in 1923, is Ralph Dolan, a young man from the provinces—Muncie, Indiana, to be exact—who elects to seek his fortune in Washington, D. C. Even in Fergusson's earliest novels, one of his favorite fictional devices is to develop in a story at least one set of opposing characters—the balanced versus the unbalanced man; the man who yields to destiny versus the man who resists it. In *Capitol Hill*, Ralph Dolan is the man of internal balance who calmly accepts life's abrupt changes and as a result receives his due reward. Ralph is a splendidly proportioned young animal "without a trace of nervousness . . . He had an excellent body—strong, stocky, hairy, round and full in chest and limb, expressing a great vitality."[1] He savors experience on every conceivable intellectual and social level; and he accepts the world's bounty—women and money especially—wherever he finds it.

Opposed to Ralph is Henry Lambert, an aspiring young writer who disapproves of Washington's carnival atmosphere and who only reluctantly manages to exist in such a state of flux. Henry, "irascible, awkward and uncomfortably plainspoken" (22), makes his living as a newspaperman but bitterly complains about the trivial events he is assigned to cover. Meanwhile, he explores Washington's monuments and relics and yearns for past glories:

As a multitude of dreamers had done before him, he turned his fancy backward and sought to create beauty out of the scanty and fabulous materials of the past. He had dreamed of a great poetic drama in which he should make the heroic days of America's beginning live again. Scenes of charm and splendor haunted his brain like beautiful ghosts, and when he sought to realize them on paper they became long rows of words among which he futilely toiled, losing his dream in a chaos of rhetoric and syntax. . . . He was painfully pregnant with poetry he could not utter. (40)

In desperation, Henry seeks to resolve his frustrations in romantic love. He marries a girl from Baltimore; but, rather than wedded bliss, he finds only a new form of bondage—the traditional middle-class trap of wife, family, and expanding indebtedness.

Ralph meets Henry, who at the time is still unmarried, not long after his arrival in Washington; and together with another young man—"Doc" Cooley, who is studying to become an osteopath—they room for a while at the local Young Men's Christian Association. When the narrative begins in 1912, Ralph is in his early twenties. For several years he had been fairly successful as traveling salesman and vagabond poker player; but, upon seeing Washington, he is filled with the ambition to "body forth his

power in the visible splendor of possession" (8). To do so, he
realizes, he must renounce the easy gratifications of his traveling
life and settle down to serious pursuits. He begins modestly
enough as a dishwasher in a small working-class diner. He is intent, however, on gaining an entry to the world of government to
which he will bring "the hunger and cunning of the purely ac-
quisitive man" (43). Because of his family's influence in Midwestern politics, Ralph arranges a meeting with an Indiana congressman, who, in exchange for Ralph's promise to help occasionally with the congressman's mail, acquires a job for him in the
folding room of the House Office Building.

From this strategic position Ralph soon locates a number of
contacts in various political circles. After a while he secures em-
ployment as secretary to Congressman James Buchanan Randall of
Texas (who appears to be a mildly satirical version of the writer's
father, Harvey Butler Fergusson). Ralph likes Randall, but he
realizes that the congressman is an anachronism whose career is
all but over. Earnestly but ineffectually, Randall crusades for a
new homestead law that will allow the Western settler a larger
plot of land; but in 1912 very little free land remained to be
claimed. In Randall's employ, Ralph becomes a master of the art
of writing evasive letters and, on his own time, an acute observer
of the trade and bluff that are the essence of Washington politics.
He also acquires, after a few months, a secretarial position with a
more promising and forward-looking congressman, Frank H.
Rauschuld.

Rauschuld, a millionaire businessman from the Midwest, believes that a stint in the House of Representatives will help advance his social and political ambitions. His pet interest is the
navy, and he puts most of his efforts into pushing for larger naval
appropriations, using in return his acquaintance with admirals and
cabinet officials to climb the Washington social ladder. He is very
conscious of public relations, and he is adept at having ideas and
quotes ready when reporters drop by his office. Indeed, he seems
to have a facile solution for almost every public problem. Rauschuld truly foreshadows the politics of the future, for he is particularly proud of one of his brainstorms: "a card index which con-
tained the name, occupation and all other available data concerning each constituent with whom the Congressman had any
dealings" (92). Much of Ralph's working time is spent in keeping this
file.

Most of Ralph's leisure moments are spent in paying court to Ethel Connor, Rauschuld's stenographer. He easily wins Ethel's affections; but, as it happens, the congressman, who also has an eye for his pretty secretary, warns Ralph, as feudal lord to retainer, that he will not tolerate an office romance. Ralph pays no heed to the warning; and, when he and Ethel are caught in the office one afternoon embracing, Ralph is immediately fired. When he sees Ethel for the last time a few days later at her brother and sister-in-law's house in the prisonlike atmosphere of a nearby suburb, she has resigned her job and says that she is about to fulfill a long-cherished dream, to travel and work abroad. Ralph realizes that, despite her plans, she still hopes he will ask her to marry him, and he is tempted. At this instant, there arises in Ralph one of those critical moments of conflicting impulses such as Fergusson describes in *Modern Man:*

Between them was that bond which unites a man and woman who have truly held each other, and which is never quite severed or forgotten. He was not a man of fine emotions, but he was bound to her by all the force of his rich vitality. And he came of a long line of men who had married and raised families. Flesh and tradition alike urged him to hold this woman who was his mate. But against them was the even stronger impulse toward freedom which was the most distinctive thing about him. . . . He had little reverence for institutions because he had not the weakling's need of their protection and support . . . . Marriage had always seemed to him a prison, and now, in an imaginative flash born of strong emotion, he suddenly visualized the reality of it. He pictured himself as the owner of a little bungalow like this one he was in, with an endless mortgage hanging over his head, with a woman holding him in legal bonds, with children perhaps—he, the lover of open roads and fresh adventures. It seemed to him suddenly that he was sitting in a trap, with a tempting bait before his nose, and that the trap might shut at any moment and hold him forever. (126–27)

Somewhat shaken, Ralph kisses Ethel goodbye and hastily departs.

Out of work, Ralph locates his friend Henry Lambert, who is now the Washington *Sun's* star reporter; and Henry helps Ralph obtain a minor job with a local newspaper. During his subsequent experiences in journalism, Ralph is introduced to a variety of newspaper types, the majority of which the author no doubt encountered during his years as a reporter. For example, there is the ineffable James Barton Otis, chief of the Washington bureau

of a large Midwestern daily: "He was, in fact, an artist of no mean
gift who, for some reason of circumstance or personality, had
been unable to find any better subject for his talent than the Re-
publican party, or any better outlet for it than a conservative
newspaper" (139). Like a great many other melancholy members
of the Washington press corps, Otis fuels his frustrated energies
with drink and bitterness.

But Ralph has a more explicit goal toward which to direct his
talents and, with his usual adroitness, quickly advances in his new
profession. He shrewdly refines the usual techniques for gleaning
and creating congressional news. More importantly, when he begins working on the side as a press agent for various special-
interest groups, he quickly ascertains the people and organizations who are willing to pay large sums of money to see certain
items in print. In his duties as newspaper reporter, Ralph meets
Jane Belden, a pretty, red-haired girl who works part-time for the
Federal Association for Woman's Suffrage. Though descended
from a socially prominent Virginia family, she is definitely an
emancipated woman; and Ralph soon becomes her companion at
many of Washington's most glittering social gatherings. He delights in the glossy surface of Jane's world, though he dislikes the
sophisticated, "arty" set with whom she occasionally associates. In
return, Jane quickly becomes contemptuous of what she considers
Ralph's philistinism; and their sometimes stormy relationship
ends abruptly when he meets Gwendolyn Shorts at one of the
parties they attend.

Gwendolyn's father, now dead, had been a cattle baron; and
her mother has brought her to Washington on a carefully planned
campaign to have her marry an Eastern millionaire or a rising
young diplomat. Ralph is dazzled by the girl's money; but, from
the beginning, he is genuinely attracted to her. Though a bit too
plump and withdrawn to make a splash in Washington high society, Gwendolyn is a buxom, healthy country girl; and "he too
was a countryman by origin—a peasant transplanted by chance,
surviving and thriving by his peasant cunning and strength. . . .
In this girl was a deep unperturbed vitality like his own, and he
felt its presence comfortably, almost unconsciously, as one feels
sunlight on an autumn day" (215). The mother is hostile to Ralph
because he is too commonplace, but Gwendolyn encourages him.
Ralph realizes that, if he hopes to marry the girl without alienat-

ing her mother, he must be cautious and exceedingly patient, perhaps wait years for the right opportunity. He is confident that he will eventually get his chance, however, because, as a friend assures him, even "a million dollars isn't enough to put a fat girl across in Washington any more especially with that ogre of a mother behind her back" (217).

Meanwhile, Ralph finds other outlets for his talents. When war breaks out in Europe, he goes to work for Colonel Melvane, one of the capital's premier lobbyists. Colonel Melvane's most important client is the National Commercial Association, a group of large manufacturing firms who have banded together to promote their viewpoint to the public and its elected representatives. For a handsome salary, he is more than happy to bring their message to the attention of Washington's politicians. The Colonel, whose background is in strikebreaking and in the management of political campaigns, is not above alarming his employers on occasion with the threat of possible radical action by Congress, a ploy which usually increases his working expenses. With war in Europe, Ralph discovers, the new watchword of the manufacturers, especially the munitions industry, is "preparedness."

When the United States finally enters the war, thanks in large measure to the activities of a bevy of lobbyists and propagandists, Ralph has "no doubt or hesitation about his proper relation to the national cataclysm. He was determined to serve his country and to serve it in some noncombative and remunerative capacity" (247). Through Colonel Melvane, he meets Colonel James Randolph Bleason, an executive with the American Red Cross. He becomes Colonel Bleason's assistant—actually his publicity agent. Ralph thinks that his new job is a sinecure; but Bleason, who fancies himself a great speaker and who has an insatiable desire for publicity, works him hard. At this point, Ralph, who has waited patiently for several years, resolves to take some final action with regard to Gwendolyn. The girl's mother, now totally discouraged, has decided to remove her to California. At the last moment, Ralph calls on Gwendolyn and proposes marriage to her; and, when she tearfully accepts, their marriage assures Ralph of the full and prosperous future he has always sought.

Near the end of the narrative Ralph runs across his old friend Henry Lambert for the last time. Before the war, Henry had abandoned his newspaper work to accept a more lucrative posi-

tion as publicity writer—propagandist, he calls it. With the out-
break of hostilities, however, he had characteristically joined the
armed forces and had been sent to fight in Europe. Now, the war
over, he is still a little bitter and uncertain about life in general.
He claims to have conquered his bemused love for the past and is
writing a novel set in the circus of contemporary Washington:
"It's a rich and beautiful spectacle, Ralph—rich in absurdity and
tragedy, in the clash and contrast of character, in the pageantry of
moving masses" (302).

Ralph, now "a young Bacchus growing stout on revelry and
good living" (290), is complacently amused by his friend's talk.
With his wife's money backing him, he has attained at age thirty
the lofty title of Executive Secretary of the National Commercial
Association, and he obviously is a young man on the make. He
has an enormous budget with which to fight the pernicious doctrines of Communism and "class legislation," and rumor has it
that the Association will support him as a candidate for Congress
from his home state of Indiana. The novel closes with Ralph's first
public speech, one delivered before the Association's annual con-
vention; he is somewhat surprised at the ease with which he
holds his audience's attention. As a result, he begins to have new
respect for himself, even to believe his own elaborate rhetoric:
"He had finished. He had made the speech of the evening. The
spontaneous crash of applause told him as much. He stood smil-
ing, high-headed, triumphant. He stood before the great of the
earth as one of them, as a leader of them. It came upon him suddenly, as an inspiration comes to a prophet, that he was an important man . . . a Great Man!" (308–09).

Capitol Hill is not, as H. L. Mencken claimed when it was
published, "the first novel of Washington life that attempts to describe genuinely typical Washingtonians and the essential
Washington."[2] The classic novel on the subject, in fact, Henry
Adams's *Democracy,* had appeared more than four decades earlier; and Fergusson's book certainly fails to reach the high literary
plane of its illustrious predecessor. On the other hand, *Capitol
Hill* has its modest virtues, and it is not simply the obscure
period piece that several recent critics have proclaimed it to be.
James K. Folsom, for instance, says that the book's portrait of the
Washington scene is no longer a recognizable picture, for the national capitol "is not so much a constant symbol of perennial

human foibles as an ever-changing example of the kaleidoscopic
quality of American life. Inevitably the novel of Washington life
loses some of its relevance with every change in the American social scene."[3]

Actually, for me, Fergusson's satirical observations of Washington politics and society are the work's most successful segments.
Many of the descriptions, far from being outdated, seem as-
tonishingly relevant to present-day Washington. For example,
the feverish activities of lobbyists, press agents and pressure
groups in the 1920's differ in degree perhaps but not in kind from
those of their descendants in the 1970's. And the essential vanity
and vulnerability of congressmen and newspapermen—indeed, of
people generally—are very much the same in any era. With a few
changes of clothing and terminology, many of the politicians and
reporters whom Ralph encounters would seem perfectly at home
in present-day Washington.

The novel's chief failing, it seems to me, is not that its setting
is dated (the same charge, after all, could be leveled at Herman
Melville's *Moby Dick* or at Nathaniel Hawthorne's *The Scarlet
Letter*), but that its narrative is loose and disjointed and that its
human participants never achieve the depth or universality required of truly believable and memorable characters. In *Capitol
Hill*, as is the case with some of the author's nonfiction, Fergusson is perhaps too ambitious: he attempts to annex too much territory; and, in trying to provide a panoramic view of all the various levels and facets of Washington life, he spreads his story
dangerously thin. The novel's plot features great breadth of
character and incident—but very little depth or direction.

The central figure, Ralph Dolan, is of course a twentieth-
century rogue, and some might agree that his adventures comprise a kind of modern picaresque novel. It is perhaps a moot
question as to whether or not the phrase "picaresque novel" is
itself a contradiction in terms, but in this particular story a given
episode usually has no relationship to episodes that precede and
follow it, except that all concern the same central character. Long
portions of the novel give no sense of progress or even change;
Ralph simply moves through a sprawling human spectacle lightly
touching a variety of people and places. Moreover, segments of the
book are often linked by extended passages of expository prose in
which the author, entertainingly but sometimes distractingly,

supplies necessary background for forthcoming incidents. In brief, *Capitol Hill* falls far short of the smoothly flowing narrative that readers normally expect in a polished work of fiction.

In addition, the book's characters, when compared with some of the writer's later studies in individual human behavior, seem unusually flat and underdeveloped. Ralph, who appears on almost every one of the work's more than three hundred pages, never becomes a really believable human being. He is merely a healthy young animal who delights in the sheer sensual pleasure of being alive and who responds eagerly to every new stimulus that life provides, but he seems never to be afflicted by that bewildering array of mental and emotional confusions with which most of us living in the actual world must daily struggle. Though the author explicitly neither approves nor disapproves of his character's behavior, he implies that Ralph, because of an admirable internal balance, reacts properly throughout most of the book to the people and events that confront him.

By the author's own argument, however, it follows that if Ralph persists in the delusions in which he indulges at the novel's end, his equilibrium will be destroyed since, according to Fergusson, a prime requisite of an individual's maintenance of balance is an ever-increasing self-knowledge. Ralph, then, as a portrait of the perfectly balanced man, is not altogether consistent or comprehensible. Moreover, compared with the depth and complexity of personality of even the most ordinary man in the street, he seems little more than a cardboard cutout. Henry Lambert, who is striving painfully to shake free from the burden of the past and to live fully in the present, seems a more realistic human being. Henry, whose Washington experiences closely parallel those of Fergusson, is undoubtedly the author's fictional self-portrait; and his dimensions as a credible personality are from the first greater than Ralph's. He does not appear often enough in the narrative, however, to become a well-developed and rounded character.

And neither do any of the myriad of other people who wander in and out of the story. They function merely as types who represent various viewpoints, both professional and social. Much as a puppeteer moves his wooden dolls, the author clearly choreographs the steps of these people, all the while offering the reader humorous comments on their behavior. The topical nature of many of these characters and the author's observations about them, I believe, make the novel seem now and then rather dated. *Capitol Hill*, therefore, is admittedly a "period piece"—but in the best sense of that term. It is, quite apart from its weaknesses of plot and character, a valuable panorama of its period—of a special time and place in American history. As a bonus, the novel's satirical criticisms of official Washington—and of the public "servants" and hangers-on who make it the fascinating community that it is—retain a measure of relevance even for the 1970's.

II *The Decline of Marriage*

Of still greater relevance to the 1970's are the characters and situations depicted in *Women and Wives*, published in 1924. While *Women and Wives*, as a fictional study of the destruction of a marriage, does not possess the depth or solidity of, say, W. D. Howells's *A Modern Instance*, it is in many ways an impressive work. Certainly its more tightly knit structure marks an advance over the formlessness of *Capitol Hill*. The story, in addition, offers a more clear-cut development of the differences between balanced and unbalanced personalities than does the earlier novel. Finally it is, as a whole, a more coherent fictional illustration of Fergusson's general philosophy, as outlined in *Modern Man*, than is *Capitol Hill*.

The early chapters of *Women and Wives* focus on Jim Royce, a student at a small Virginia college. Jim, a moody youth, often gloomily wanders at night through the surrounding countryside and during the day spends his leisure hours reading in the college library. He has ambitions to become a writer, but he thinks of "art in any form as something sweet and lovely—a dainty icing on the good cake of life."[4] He courts a girl from Richmond named Catherine Larue; and, following graduation from college, he convinces Catherine that she should marry him. Each of the prospective partners is, in his own way, self-centered; and each entertains the illusion of marriage as idyllic and sustained happiness. Catherine is not sure she loves Jim, but she more or less drifts into a commitment to marry. Once committed, she is preoccupied with the traditional forms—the engagement party, the invitations, gifts, and the wedding ceremony—that her family puts her through; as a result, she has little time to contemplate what marriage will really be like.

On their honeymoon, the couple's sexual adjustment to each

other is poor from the outset. At first, Catherine is cool to Jim's advances and professes to be repulsed by the idea of life as "a pageant of sex" (59). Their difficulties multiply when they settle down to everyday life. Because Jim's father is a retired newspaperman who retains a vestige of Washington influence, Jim acquires a minor position in the publicity office of a government bureau, and he hopes to use this steady job as the basis for launching a career in journalism and literature. He and Catherine locate an apartment in Washington, but their life together remains trying: they sleep in separate bedrooms, and only occasionally find any joy or contentment with each other. They have very little social life, and their attempts at conversation quickly end when one or the other picks up a magazine or book and a wall of silence descends between them. On a few rare evenings their embraces "bridge the gap of constraint and boredom" (82), but Catherine in particular is appalled by the never-ending monotony and tedium that pervade their lives: "Here married life seemed to stretch before her endlessly—a desert of monotonous, meaningless difficulties" (114). Like a modern-day Hester Prynne, she discovers an outlet for her tensions and frustrated creativity in sewing and in dress-designing.

The best moments of Catherine and Jim's marriage occur when they are closest to nature—afternoons spent along the Potomac River and, after they acquire an automobile, a summer vacation of camping in the Virginia mountains. But even the restorative powers of nature cannot prevent a return to the old routine of boredom and restlessness. For his part, Jim finds his job to be mostly drudgery, though his superiors quickly come to depend on his good mind and adept pen. A friend advises him to quit and go out on his own; for most employees in government offices, the friend warns, once they have held their positions a few years, ordinarily stay until they rot. Jim listens attentively but makes no promises; instead, he regresses to childhood daydreams, seeking escape through fantasies of travel and adventure. With liquor and with volumes by Kipling and Conrad, he spends his evenings vaguely planning a sailing trip to the tropics. In actuality, his only travels are the occasions when he takes the car and drives through nearby rural areas of Virginia and Maryland, guiltily returning home long after midnight.

One spring day an acquaintance in another office asks Jim to go swimming with him. When they reach the car, Jim discovers that two girls from his friend's office are to accompany them. Jim is reluctant but eventually decides to go along. The girl who becomes his companion for the afternoon is blond, pretty, and something of a tease; and they enjoy several hours of innocent gaity. When he returns home, he finds an angry Catherine, who by accident had seen the car pass on a nearby street with Jim sitting beside "that horrid little blond" (130). Contrite, Jim begs her forgiveness. He is overwhelmed by guilt and remorse, which the author, commenting freely on his character's emotions, calls "spiritual constipation. The strong and the free sin blithely and forgive themselves, but little men sin miserably and stew in the juices of regret" (131).

Beneath his guilt, however, Jim vaguely realizes that his marriage has become a trap. A basic requirement of personal autonomy, he concludes, is freedom of association; and marriage by its nature severely restricts such freedom. Wandering in the city zoo, he stops near the cage of a wolf which has been recently contributed to the collection by a Montana forest ranger. The friendly wolf has obviously been raised as a pet, for it appears actually to welcome its imprisonment. The scene before him strikes Jim as the very emblem of the marriage structure. Shortly thereafter, the blond girl, whose name is Fanny Miller, is transferred to Jim's department. Since Jim is intensely dissatisfied with his marriage and since Fanny is in revolt against her family's restrictive morality, an affair between them seems inevitable; indeed, they are soon meeting clandestinely in a friend's apartment.

Catherine's experiences lead, step by step, to a similar and even more far-reaching education. One night at a party she and Jim meet John Strome, who had been a college classmate of Jim's. Strome, originally from the Kansas prairies, has traveled widely since his college days; and, as an archaeologist with the Smithsonian Institution, he has participated in a variety of challenging expeditions and lives, in short, the kind of life Jim only dreams of living. Catherine is immediately attracted to Strome, and they begin meeting for lunch in a downtown tea-room. He flatters her intellect, not with "mushy" talk, but by discussing world problems with her. As they are parting outside the tea-room one afternoon, they are astonished to encounter Jim walking down the street. Though Catherine tells him they had met accidentally, Jim is suspicious; and Catherine resolves to terminate her meetings with Strome: "But her virtue gave her no

pleasure. . . . Vaguely she realized that cowardice and the desire
for peace lay at the root of her fortitude. She had surrendered
another block of her personal liberty, but she had done it with
bad grace, in a mood of rebellion" (143). She subconsciously recognizes that, as the author explains in *Modern Man*, much human
behavior which on the surface seems courageous and moral is
prompted, not by ethical principle or a need to do good, but by
fear and the pressures of society. The last time Catherine sees
Strome in Washington, he tells her he has decided to accept a
position as assistant curator of anthropology in a large New York
museum, and, with a knowing look, he asks her to come see him
if she is ever in that city.

Catherine's discontentment intensifies when she begins reading
books on psychoanalysis and talking with "liberated" women
friends. As a result, the last straw to her is Jim's promotion
among a group of his acquaintances of an all-male camping trip on
the Potomac. Catherine, who had wanted to use his vacation
otherwise, is angry; they argue, but Jim, determined to at least
partially fulfill his fantasies, goes anyway. When Jim leaves,
Catherine hesitates briefly, then resolves to make an immediate
break with her husband. She packs her things and catches a train
for New York where, for a time, she is lonely and uncertain and
even thinks at one point of returning to Washington and Jim. At
this crucial moment she meets an old friend, Marion Conway,
who is delighted to initiate Catherine into a new and exciting environment.

Marion is something of a rebel and an adventuress, and she
plunges Catherine into a world that seems as strange to her as

the fauna of Australia must have seemed to the first explorers. These
people were all rebels and very self-conscious ones. The thing they all
seemed to have in common was that they had come from somewhere
else in search of freedom and achievement. They were all renegades
from the vast hinterlands of middle-class respectability, and they took
pride and delight in that role. They made a clever art of saying things
obscene, blasphemous and heretical. They drank gin, smoked cigarettes,
danced with both arms about each other, and sometimes even kissed in
public. They mocked and flouted every propriety. . . . They were almost
as conceited about their immoralities as a Baptist deacon is about his virtues. They mouthed their heresies with all the unction their fathers had
brought to platitudes. (285)

At first, Catherine feels out of place among such people, but soon gets into the swing of things. She enrolls herself in a course in dress-designing at the Metropolitan School of Applied Art, where she discovers that she has genuine talent as a designer; and, for the first time in her life, she enjoys feelings of usefulness and self-worth. One day, passing the museum where Strome works, she obeys an impulse to enter. She is prepared to accept Strome as her lover without fear or shame, and he of course welcomes her joyously. "Life," Catherine tells herself, "gives you what you want if you dare to take it. Life asks of you but the courage to live" (290).

Jim, for his part, does not fare nearly so well. When he finds that Catherine has left him, he is at first consumed by jealousy, certain that she has fled with another man. Then he becomes sick with loneliness; he begins drinking too much and even contemplates suicide. When the initial shock wears off, he gradually realizes that his new freedom will permit him to do many of those things he has dreamed of doing: writing, taking that long-delayed cruise to the Caribbean, retiring to a place in the country. But Jim lacks "that last desperate fling of energy and courage which is necessary to overcome the awful inert indifference that life opposes to self-assertion" (300). On a streetcar one afternoon he spies Fanny Miller sitting a few seats in front of him; and, since he has not seen Fanny for some time, he speaks to her. With a little coaxing, she agrees to go with him to his apartment; Fanny shrewdly recognizes that she now has an opportunity to capture Jim for herself. She immediately becomes possessive, and begins tidying up Jim's disorderly flat; she tells him she loves him and yields herself willingly; but, when she caresses him as if he were a baby, Jim both requires and resents the awesome force of Fanny's maternal affection. In her moment of triumph, he can only acquiesce timidly to her superior strength: "Whether he married her or not, he knew he would never escape her. She was not like Catherine. She would not discover his weakness and turn away. She would love and cherish and admire, and she would never set him free. She would bind him tight . . . In this moment of love, which filled her cup so full, he knew certainly that, for him, no love could be enough" (310).

Though the sense of an authorial presence manipulating characters and passing judgment on their actions remains strong in the book, the narrative current of *Women and Wives* is considerably more forceful than that of *Capitol Hill*. To be sure, parts of the work ramble; and the writer continues occasionally to offer his musings on a variety of subjects; but, in general, the plot is straightforward and skillfully constructed. The basic structure of the book is a familiar one to readers of American fiction: the crossing pattern described by two lives moving in opposite directions. (Henry James's *The Ambassadors* and Ernest Hemingway's "The Short Happy Life of Francis Macomber" come to mind as works that, in part at least, employ a similar structure.) In the beginning, Jim is a promising college graduate who hopefully anticipates marriage and a career, while Catherine is a naive and uncertain girl. As the plot progresses, Jim steadily descends until, at the end dependent for emotional support on a witless creature whom he is powerless to control, he reaches his nadir; but Catherine grows, hesitantly but surely, and eventually develops into a happy, richly fulfilled woman. At some indeterminate point in the story their courses cross, touch briefly, and then diverge—after which the reader slowly becomes convinced that their relationship is doomed and that only the details of disintegration remain to be worked out. The circumstance that the high point of Jim's life is shown in the first chapter and his utter degradation in the last has been criticized as inconsistent and unsatisfactory and as, therefore, a weakness in the novel.[5] Considering the plot pattern and character types the author is using, however, it seems to me both right and inevitable.

Women and Wives is also superior to *Capitol Hill* in that its major characters are believable human beings. As in the second novel, much of the narrative tension in the first springs from the author's juxtaposition of opposing character types—that is, balanced versus unbalanced characters. One opposition obviously is that of Jim Royce versus John Strome; for Jim is weak and emotionally unbalanced, and any equilibrium he achieves must be imposed from without. Under stress, he exhibits regressive tendencies by returning to childhood habits of thought and behavior. He dreams of escape and freedom; but, when his chance for freedom occurs, he is unable to seize it. Large numbers of men, Fergusson says in *Modern Man*, elect to be slaves and would not know what to do with genuine personal autonomy even if it were granted them; like Jim and like the pet wolf he sees at the zoo, they prefer the security of the cage to the uncertainty of freedom.

Strome, on the other hand, is cool and serene, a natural leader. He knows what he wants from life, and he enjoys both the pursuit and the attainment of his goals. He is sure-footed in a sometimes unstable environment because he understands himself thoroughly and has therefore acquired internal balance. But Strome, like Ralph Dolan, is not realistically developed; he is an ideal, a standard by which the behavior of others is measured; and, like all ideal characters, his personality is thin and unconvincing. Fortunately for the novel's esthetic effectiveness, however, he is a minor rather than a major character; indeed, he is used mainly as a stage prop.

The story's central figures, Catherine and Jim Royce, also form a set of opposing characters in that one achieves equilibrium and peace of mind while the other becomes increasingly less capable of functioning as an independent agent. They are realistic human beings not because of what they represent but because they suffer, weep, scream, hesitate to act, and are subject to doubt and uncertainty—to all the mental and emotional ailments that flesh is heir to. The reader understands, perhaps even identifies with, these two people. The course of seemingly trivial events, the small compromises on the one hand and the assertions of courage on the other, that leads these characters to their ultimate fates is both fascinating and instructive. Moreover, the murderous squeeze in which Jim and Catherine find themselves—the death throes of a moribund marriage—is a nearly universal human situation and is easily recognizable, even by those who have not experienced it firsthand. Certainly this grim setting is as relevant today as it was half a century ago.

The marriage arrangement and the reasons why it seems less and less feasible in the modern world are the author's principal thematic concerns in *Women and Wives*. In both *Modern Man* and *People and Power,* Fergusson assesses the declining influence of the family as one of the most significant developments in twentieth-century American society. According to Fergusson, the patriarchal family structure, in primitive and Medieval societies, served an important social, even political, function; for it not only afforded its members guidance and support; but stabilized society generally. But in a transient, rootless ambience such as modern-day America, a stable family quickly becomes an anachronism;

and one of the traditional motives for marriage is thereby removed. When many couples live, as do Jim and Catherine, in a series of rented urban apartments, they are divorced from the land and the traditions it nurtures—and are therefore separated from the factors that made the patriarchal family possible. Additionally, Fergusson believes, there is no longer a social necessity for a man and woman to have children, a circumstance that in the past provided .a strong impetus toward marriage. At one point, Catherine believes that her having a baby might strengthen her and Jim's relationship; but a friend argues that the world is becoming overpopulated, and there is no sense adding to the approaching crisis. Moreover, the friend continues, it is folly to try to shore up a crumbling marriage with children, who themselves become victims. Catherine is easily convinced by her friend's rational argument. When modern man, then, is deprived of the need to procreate on the one hand and to establish a rigid family structure on the other, he has only one reason to marry: romantic love. "And," says Fergusson, "the one sure thing about love is that it dies" (295). Under current conditions, the author concludes, marriage is no longer a strong and vital institution; and his parable of Catherine and Jim Royce is intended as a practical illustration of that conclusion.

Women and Wives—as are most of the author's fictions to one degree or another—is a philosophical novel in that its themes are based largely on ideas and assumptions that are explicitly stated and developed in *Modern Man* (and to a lesser extent in *People and Power*). Any philosophy, it seems to me, when pushed too hard, becomes obtrusive in a work of fiction and dilutes that work's overall effectiveness. Indeed, a recurring defect of Fergusson's fiction is a sometimes unbecoming persistence and cocksureness: he often tries rhetorically to bully the reader into accepting a cluster of debatable premises that are scarcely as self-evident as he claims. But it is a tribute to the writer's artistry and craftsmanship that much of his fiction—*Women and Wives*, for instance—effortlessly transcends the questionable assumptions on which it stands. Whether or not the average reader agrees with those assumptions, he cannot fail, I think, to appreciate the intensely realistic portrayal of Catherine and Jim Royce; for he will recognize in their joy and agony, in their triumphs and defeats, something of his own experience.

CHAPTER 4

Modern Man in the Southwest

A S the preceding chapters make clear, Harvey Fergusson was concerned all his adult life with problems of state and society that are national in scope and with principles of human behavior that go far beyond the narrow limits of class or region. Yet from the first he was labeled as a sectional writer. His Southwestern heritage and rearing and the fact that a majority of his novels (eight of the ten) are set in his native region combine, in the minds of many, to relegate him to that minor category of American literature: the regional novelist. At one time—in the 1920's and 1930's, when "regionalism" was a popular mode of American thought and criticism—the label was probably helpful in bringing Fergusson to the attention of many readers and reviewers. Today, when "regional" is a term of contempt sometimes used by critics to dismiss summarily a book or writer, Fergusson's reputation as a regionalist, I believe, has obscured his very real achievements from the ken of most students of American literature.

Every writer has his home country: it may be large cities—and they too are, in part, Fergusson's country—or it may be an exotic, isolated region like the American Southwest. In the imagination of every writer there lives that "postage stamp of soil" (as William Faulkner called his Yoknapatawpha County) where the drama of all life and all time is played out in microcosm. Fergusson's "postage stamp of soil" is northern New Mexico —Albuquerque in particular, but also a triangle of mountains and desert, the points of which are Albuquerque to the south, Taos to the north, and Las Vegas to the northeast. Here men live with the immensity and grandeur of the land, and their destinies are unquestionably affected by that land. But men, whether they live in New York or Albuquerque, are subject to essentially the same fears and appetites, the same human capacities and limitations. And during the last few decades, of course, even the most remote corners of the United States have been irrevocably changed by technological developments, by advances in transportation and communication: as a result, these areas have been brought more into the mainstream of the nation's social and cultural flow.

Several of Fergusson's novels are set in the twentieth-century Southwest; and, though he was critical in these books of the region's backward and inflexible code of morality and behavior, he seemed to recognize that, even in the 1920's and 1930's, times were rapidly changing. These novels suggest that, on the whole, the modern-day Southwesterner is not much different from the "modern man" who inhabits Washington or New York, the settings in *Capitol Hill* and *Women and Wives*, respectively. Fergusson during his long life came to know both environments intimately—the spacious Southwest and the large cities of the East—and a work of personal history which links the two and provides some basis for comparing them is *Home in the West*, Fergusson's autobiography.

I   *A Representative Life*

Home in the West: An Inquiry into My Origins was published in 1944 when Fergusson was fifty-four years old. It is partly autobiography, partly (as the subtitle indicates) a retrospective inquiry into the writer's ancestral heritage, and partly the account of one man's halting and sometimes painful education. The writer was born in the nineteenth century and was nurtured on nineteenth-century values and beliefs, and only with considerable difficulty was he able to teach himself to become a "modern man." As the story of an educational process, the book properly ends when the education is complete; chronologically, the final event in the narrative is a frank description of the author's sexual initiation during World War I when he was in his late twenties.

As autobiography, then, *Home in the West* is a fragmentary but valuable source. It provides a full and fascinating account of the life and times of the author's maternal grandfather, considerably less information concerning his paternal grandfather, a memorable portrait of his father, and only a few sketchy descriptions of his mother. With admirable thoroughness, Fergusson tells the reader what it was like to grow up in an isolated Southwestern town around the turn of the century; he also introduces him to the bizarre world of a small Southern college during the years of 1907 to 1911; and he leaves him with a view of pre-World War I Washington, D. C., as seen through the eyes of a young newspaper reporter.

Throughout *Home in the West* Fergusson is commendably honest concerning himself and his motivations, and part of his honesty is an admission that his life, as such, is perhaps not worthy of being memorialized in a full-scale autobiography. But he believes—correctly, I think—that his experiences, rather than being simply haphazard occurrences in an individual life, are representative of a widespread social and intellectual movement during the early decades of the twentieth century. He therefore selects and emphasizes—especially in the last half of the book —those events in his autobiography which seem significant, in one way or another, to many more lives than just his own. "I have tried," he says in the preface, "to combine the story of a period and a region with that of a man."[1] Apparently, then, the book should be read on those three tiers of descending importance: period, region, individual man.

Fergusson begins, however, with the region, perhaps the most personal and unusual element in his experience. Wallace Stegner, in his essay "Born a Square: The Westerner's Dilemma,"[2] suggests that the writer from the American West is in certain respects different from other writers and that much of the difference springs from the sheer magnitude of the physical environment in which he was reared. Though hardly a typical Western writer, Fergusson, by his testimony in *Home in the West*, seems to support Stegner's thesis. The first chapter of his autobiography is entitled "Home Is a Country," and it begins with a statement of attitude: "To me, home is less a town or a house or a society than a region—this piece of earth. . . . I must begin with this emotion because it is a primary fact of my experience and seems to have determined the pattern of my life" (4). He describes a place that as a child he invested with special meaning—a bluff south of Albuquerque which overlooks the Rio Grande: "As I survey this scene of my oldest memories I always feel that I have come back to the one changeless thing I know. In a world of flux this time-defying landscape gives me a feeling of peace and reassurance, lends life a continuity it would otherwise lack. 'Only the earth lasts forever,' is an old Mexican proverb, and only the earth always takes you back, dead or alive" (4).

As a boy, Fergusson wandered over hundreds of square miles of northern New Mexico; ostensibly, his wanderings were hunting forays, but he in reality was seeking, in the beauty and discipline of nature, a refuge from home town and family. As is true of many people who live close to the earth, his relationship with nature became the wellspring of feelings that might almost be called religious: "I am convinced," he writes, "that it [a love for the earth] is one of the ancient and recurrent human experiences and one of the permanent sources of human faith in life" (151). In some people, Fergusson continues, this love engenders "a feeling of reassurance that sometimes rises to ecstasy because it sets the individual free from all fear of death and doubt of life. It is not a thought in the mind but a song in the blood" (160).

Not surprisingly, many characters in the writer's fiction are similarly suffused, in the presence of nature, with almost mystical emotions. In *Women and Wives,* for instance, Jim Royce, on a camping trip along the Potomac, discovers in the forests that line the river's banks a peace and contentment that he cannot find in wife, job, or urban apartment. Departing on one occasion from a sylvan glade where he had experienced a mood of blissful content, "He turned and went quietly out of the forest as a penitent goes from church, with his soul purged and at peace" (274). Like Jim Royce, Fergusson recognized only one house of worship: the blue dome of nature.

As a youth, the author dreamed of becoming a rancher or forest ranger and of living a happy and useful life in his native region. He gradually realized, however, as he reached maturity, that his destiny lay not in the red earth of New Mexico but in the din and bustle of large cities—settings more likely than Albuquerque to yield the intellectual fulfillment he sought, as well as a modicum of material success. When he moved to Washington and later to New York and California, he was fascinated by the human spectacle that surrounded him; but he also felt a sense of loss in that he no longer had immediate access to the lonely grandeur of mountains and desert. "During the years I lived in the East," he writes in *Home in the West,* "nostalgia was the most constant emotion of my life" (5). When it became financially possible, he began returning to New Mexico during his summers for weeks and even months at a stretch. For years, he arranged his affairs so that he might live and work during the winters in cities on one of the two coasts, while spending summers in the Southwest: "I spent much of my life leaving this country and returning, traveling a hundred thousand miles, having always the spirit of an itinerant or a camper. This going and coming was long the rhythm of my existence" (5).

This cycle of escape and return, which Fergusson perceives as the dominant pattern of his own life, also shapes the course of many of his fictional characters' lives. Escape of whatever kind, the author tells us in *Modern Man,* is a regressive tendency, an attempt to retreat into the past; and one form of escape is to retire to a natural world that has not yet been touched by human society or technology. If an individual lives in the society of men, he must expect to live in an environment of ceaseless change; nature, on the other hand—especially so imposing a natural scene as the Southwestern landscape which the writer, in a passage quoted above, describes as his boyhood retreat—seems ordered and changeless; therefore, it appears to offer a refuge from the uncertainties of a fluctuating society. Fergusson believes that every man, when fatigued and discouraged, entertains escapist impulses.

And it is altogether proper, the author concedes, to seek some outlet for those impulses; in his own case, for instance, annual visits to New Mexico proved a healthful and restorative tonic which allowed him to return to his work with renewed zest and vigor. But the individual must recognize that permanent escape is a denial of destiny and results in personal stagnation and disintegration. Concerning Fergusson's own periodic returns to nature, he says: "I always felt clearly that my retreat was nothing better than a return to the past and to childhood, that my real business was elsewhere and especially in cities. . . . So I always went back to my perspiring struggle, whether in Washington, New York, or Hollywood, and always stood it as long as I could" (168). In the novels, the successful characters, in Fergusson's view, are those who, when necessary, find a temporary refuge—usually nature, though occasionally something else—and later return revitalized to their function within the social mechanism. The failures are those who are so weak and unbalanced that they cannot maintain their equilibrium in a world of flux and must withdraw permanently to some kind of stable but enervating environment.

Fergusson, however, was shaped not only by the land where he was born, but also by the times in which he lived. Indeed, the principal significance of *Home in the West,* it seems to me, is that it is the personal record of a crucial period in American history —the decades between 1890 and 1920. During those years, Fergusson believes, the nation was undergoing a profound social and ethical revolution. The social revolution had to do mainly with a large increase in population—and the accompanying growing pains—combined with a rapid changeover from a rural to a predominantly urban society. During the nineteenth century, of course, the distance between large cities and rural areas seemed infinitely greater than the mere miles that separated them. Because of the rural and small-town people's suspicions of the "wicked city" on the one hand and the urban dweller's contempt for the country bumpkin on the other, divisions arose within the nation which have not been wholly resolved to this day. The split, the author believes, actually widened during the decades immediately following the turn of the century; then, as a result of technological advances, it began to close somewhat.

When Fergusson was born in 1890, Albuquerque was still little more than a frontier town—a railroad town, to be specific—which was "self-contained and isolated in a way that no small town is now" (121). Its social structure, the writer tells us, was rigid and well-organized; and there were a great many meaningless social forms and engagements that the individual had to observe. Those bold enough to refuse to conform to the town's values and traditions were dismissed as cranks and misfits, despite the fact that Albuquerque's citizens around the turn of the century clung tenaciously to a belief in self-reliance and individualism. Their version of self-reliance, however, was closer to that of Benjamin Franklin than of Thoreau. "I accepted," writes the author, "the philosophy of thrift and hustle but I knew instinctively that I would never practice it" (121). A sensitive child growing up in such an environment might be expected to develop rather strong anti-social feelings; and such feelings were indeed the source, as we have noted, of many of Fergusson's extended hunting expeditions. Later, as did large numbers of talented and alienated young people from all sections of the nation, he became an exile, leaving his home country for the more rewarding and exciting environment of large Eastern cities.

In *Home in the West*, after much reflection and soul-searching, Fergusson is able, if not to forgive his home town, at least to understand it. He also admits that, in the years that have passed since he was a boy in Albuquerque, the chasm between small-town America as it exists in reality and as he wishes it to be has narrowed considerably. This circumstance, he asserts, is in large measure the result of improved technology. Better transportation and communication have hastened the leveling process and have brought Americans, wherever they live, closer to their fellow citizens. Even in the 1920's the ubiquitous automobile was working a radical change in the nation's way of life: "the motor car and the paved road created a new personal freedom," Fergusson believes, and served to break down both geographical barriers and traditional social patterns (104).

Accompanying the social revolution chronicled in *Home in the West,* there has occurred in America in the first half of the twentieth century, the author contends, a concomitant ethical revolution—and its most apparent result has been a widespread shift in sexual beliefs and mores. As an illustrative example, the writer cites his own evolving attitudes toward women and his belated sexual initiation. In late nineteenth-century Albuquerque, as in most small towns of that era, young men were taught that there are two kinds of women: those to be worshipped and those to be enjoyed. As an abstraction, woman was "at once an ideal of purity and the chief cause and instrument of sin" (177). The respective citadels of these two kinds of women were the traditional home and the house of prostitution. It was not uncommon for small towns around the turn of the century to have extensive "red light districts" where even the most respectable male citizens occasionally sought pleasure and an evening's refuge from their angelic wives and daughters. The persistence, the writer contends, of these false notions concerning the nature of woman has created a backlog of inhibitions and psychological suffering that even today has not been wholly relieved.

In Fergusson's case, he was indoctrinated from an early age in such mistaken assumptions; and they were predictably the source of much pain and confusion. As a boy and young man, he was, he writes, "by turns and after a fashion a dream-bound idealist, a Puritan, a prude, and a professing libertine, so that I had a varied experience of mood and viewpoint if a somewhat limited one of delight" (175). Around members of the opposite sex he was from the first shy and awkward, and even as a young reporter in Washington he remained firmly shackled by his inhibitions. During World War I, he met in Washington a girl named Alice —apparently very much like Jane Belden in *Capitol Hill*—who was a Suffragette and a woman of enlightened attitudes. But the two were rather uneasy with each other; for, while each was a professing rebel, he was also a practicing puritan. When their relationship was finally consummated one evening, it was, for both, an experience of immense physical and psychological release; and Fergusson contends that the event, trivial as it may seem to the average reader, symbolically freed him from his sexual misconceptions and liberated him from the bonds of the past. Though he admits to some vestigial reluctance to speak of himself in this regard, the writer believes that his case history is so representative of many similar experiences in the early decades of the twentieth century that it possesses a measure of general significance. "During the First World War," he writes, "and the years immediately after it, something like a moral revolution took place in America, and it coincided exactly with a revolution in my own mental and emotional being" (213).

Fergusson's pre-occupation with his personal sexual history is reflected in various ways in his fiction. For one thing, he is probably the first writer from the American West to take any realistic notice of the physical relationships between men and women. "Take all the pioneer women in the chronicles," the late J. Frank Dobie once said; "not a single one of them has a breast, or a flank, or a perfume in the mouth."[3] And indeed almost all early writings about the American West and Southwest, including fiction, were extremely reticent about sex. Fergusson, so far as I am aware, was the first Western writer to recognize publicly that sexual union is one of the basic human drives and honestly and openly to confront this fact in his books. To jaded readers of the 1970's, this statement probably sounds rather innocent—even naive—but we must remember that, when Fergusson began writing, the influence of the Genteel Tradition had not been altogether eradicated; and it should perhaps be added that a kind of "genteel tradition" persisted in Western and Southwestern fiction considerably longer than it did in American fiction generally. Many of Fergusson's books, in any event, contain accounts of sexual episodes. In compliance with the fashions of the time, they are never explicitly described, the author always maintaining a tasteful restraint; but one commendable result of this approach is that the descriptions occasionally, especially in the sketches of those decisive meetings that advance the workings of destiny, rise almost to the level of poetry.

But, despite Fergusson's honest and sometimes lyrical use of sexual themes in his novels, he seems never really to have escaped the handicaps imposed by his upbringing. Unfortunately, those erroneous beliefs concerning female anatomy and psychology, which he renounced in his personal life, found their way into much of his fiction with the result that most of his women characters are little more than embodiments of male fantasy or prejudice. Usually they are merely "sex objects" in the male characters' daydreams and often they are odd creatures whom the men view as competitors and enemies rather than as companions to be loved and trusted. In fact, only two women in his books —Catherine Royce in *Women and Wives* and, to a lesser degree, Ruth Bruck in *Hot Saturday*—have any depth or reality as human beings.

In his failure to create believable female characters Fergusson is not, of course, alone, since most male American writers suffer from a similar myopia—a weakness that Fergusson's meticulous detailing of his early misconceptions perhaps in part explains. For example, it is now a commonplace among critics of American literature that even so accomplished a writer as Ernest Hemingway was almost pitifully inept in drawing credible female characters; his women are either exemplary heroines or, to use the vernacular, "bitches," and in neither category do the individual female characters become anything more than stereotypes. In the presence of women most male American writers seem confused, awed, and somewhat resentful; and in this regard Fergusson is no exception. His fictional world, like that of most of his male colleagues, remains an essentially masculine one. Certainly he appears much surer of his footing when he is exploring the consciousness of hairy-chested males than when he is attempting to account for the sometimes mystifying behavior of women.

Home in the West, in any event, is a first-rate autobiography.

Though when it appeared it was greeted by generally unfavorable reviews (and by some definitely hostile ones),[4] the book, I believe, might well serve as a model for future writers who wish to try their hands at recounting personal experiences, one of the most difficult and demanding of writing assignments. The task of the autobiographer, it seems to me, is to present himself as a noteworthy, even singular personality, while simultaneously demonstrating that his life is in some way representative of the age in which he lived. When this delicate balance is upset, autobiographical writing tends to become either mere personal aggrandizement on the one hand or a form of social reportage on the other.

Fergusson, with superlative skill, manages throughout his book to maintain a perfect equilibrium. He observes himself and his behavior with an admirable detachment and reveals, however reluctantly, as much of the truth as seems relevant to his purpose. He shows himself to be, like most of his fellows, an individual who struggles through life with considerable difficulty and not a little pain, who wins his share of victories but who in the end assesses himself as having been only partially successful. But the reader who finishes *Home in the West* has, in addition to many insights into the author's mind and motives, a greatly enlarged knowledge of an American epoch—the years immediately preceding and following the turn of the present century—and this knowledge, I believe, is the most valuable aid the autobiography offers toward an understanding of much of the writer's fiction.

II *Primitive Man in the Southwest*

For readers unfamiliar with the region and the times, then, *Home in the West* is an excellent introduction to the early twentieth-century Southwest. Four of Fergusson's novels—*The Blood of the Conquerors, Hot Saturday, Footloose McGarnigal,* and *The Life of Riley*—fill in the picture that is sketched out in the autobiography; for these works develop many of the themes and areas of interest which the author, of necessity, only alludes to or briefly summarizes in *Home in the West. The Blood of the Conquerors,* the writer's first published novel, was composed during his spare time while he was still employed as a newspaper reporter, and was published in 1921. A well-written, thought-provoking book—certainly an auspicious beginning for a young novelist—it clearly sets forth many of the subjects that Fergusson would be concerned with throughout his writing career. According to his sister Erna, the author described in the novel's central character, Ramon Delcasar, "a playmate, a schoolmate with whom he vied for his first girl."[5] In Ramon, the novelist also discovered a useful persona through which to examine one of the Southwest's most pressing social problems—the causes and consequences of prejudice.

The Blood of the Conquerors, writes Cecil Robinson in *With the Ears of Strangers: The Mexican in American Literature,* is a reliable historical portrait of "the old Mexican families of the Albuquerque region in full decay and in the final stages of what was to become an almost total dispossession."[6] When the narrative begins about 1912—in a town that is never named but is obviously Albuquerque—Ramon Delcasar is the last descendant of a family of *ricos,* proud Spanish aristocrats who had once ruled a large portion of New Mexico's land and people. Fergusson, through research and personal observation, very early acquired a detailed and sympathetic knowledge of such families as the Delcasars; and descriptions of their intricate familial operations are among the more impressive features of several of his Southwestern novels. Don Solomon, the eighteenth-century founder of the Delcasar clan, had owned "not only lands and herds but also men and women. The *peons* who worked his lands were his possessions as much as were his horses. He had them beaten when they offended him and their daughters were his for the taking."[7]

The Delcasars, according to Fergusson, like most of the *rico* families, had from the beginning weakened their aristocratic lineage by mingling their blood with that of the native Indian population. Then, when the Anglos overran the country in the mid-nineteenth century, bringing with them a new law and a new social ethic, their disintegration was assured. Most members of *rico* families, by the close of the century, had "either died, departed or sunk from sight into the mass of the peasantry" (24). Anglos, of course, usually made no attempt to distinguish between descendants of aristocrats and those of the peons; all were simply "Mexicans."

With the advent of the twentieth century, the only member of the ancient house of Delcasar who retains any of the family's once enormous wealth is Ramon's Uncle Diego; and he is a pitiful symbol of his family's degeneration. Though he had once been an active and adventurous man, Diego now thinks only of the past and longs for the days before the Anglos came. He dissipates himself and his wealth in idle pleasure-seeking and seems not to care very much what happens to himself or to his fortune. Diego has entered into a loose partnership with a real-estate agent named MacDougall, who, as it turns out, is systematically fleecing him: MacDougall loans the old man money and, when he is unable to repay it, forecloses on the property put up as collateral. For the "gringos" Ramon feels "a cold hostility—a sense of antagonism and difference—but it was his senile and fatuous uncle, the type of his own defeated race, whom he despised" (32).

Ramon, who is Diego's sole heir, is sent to law school in St. Louis, where he unexpectedly encounters a great deal of prejudice; and, though he has no real interest in the law, he reacts to his classmates' bias by competing fiercely for scholastic honors. When Ramon's legal training is completed, he returns to his native town where he gets a job as a minor functionary in the office of an Anglo lawyer. At the office, he spends his days on a variety of trivial, unfulfilling tasks; his leisure time is made miserable by an ambiguous social position: "his social footing was a peculiarly uncertain thing for the reason that he was a Mexican. . . . In the little southwestern town where he had lived all his life, his social position was ostensibly of the highest. He was spoken of as belonging to an old and prominent family. Yet he knew of mothers who carefully guarded their daughters from the peril of falling in love with him, and most of his boyhood fights had started when some one called him 'a damned Mexican' or a 'greaser' " (7–8).

The crucial event of Ramon's life occurs when he meets and falls in love with Julia Roth, a rich Eastern girl whose family disapproves of her seeing him. Julia is fond of Ramon—indeed, admits that she loves him—but she seems totally incapable of acting independently. She does not wish to offend her family, nor does she want to hurt Ramon: so she does nothing. For his part Ramon, who has never been particularly ambitious, decides that, in order to establish a basis on which to deal with Julia's family, he must begin amassing money and power. This quest for love and power that is triggered by Ramon's meeting Julia richly illustrates many aspects of the writer's philosophy of life. As Fergusson indicates in *Modern Man*, for instance, it is extremely important that the fully functioning individual, rather than just thinking or hoping or dreaming, find some means of *action*, some outlet for his impulses and reflections. The only requisites for action, the writer claims, are a motivating impulse and a clearly defined objective. Most of the author's fictional characters, consequently, labor and strive to reach some desired goal; it may be the accumulation of money, land, and power or, on a less grandiose level, merely the infiltration of a small town's feudal society. But, whatever it is, the goal is both a means of self-proof and, since men naturally desire to work for the attainment of a difficult objective, an end in itself.

Fergusson's affirmation, in his personal philosophy, of the necessity to work and struggle may well be a vestige of that Puritan ethic—that religion of "thrift and hustle," as he calls it in *Home in the West*—implanted in him as a youth. Fergusson does not, however, subscribe to the Puritan belief that material possessions are, in themselves, a measure of God's favor. That a character's best efforts may not result in material or financial success is, the author asserts, of no real significance; for destiny may dictate what, to the world at large, looks like failure. Even the lives of great men are rarely unbroken chains of successes, and the average person's destiny, he writes in *Home in the West*, "is normally both an ordeal and a defeat, even though it has incidental triumphs" (77). An individual's destiny requires only that he continue to struggle; the individual denies his destiny, as we have seen, when he admits defeat and attempts permanently to withdraw into some kind of stable but unchallenging environment.

In the case of Ramon, his love for Julia soon becomes the guiding impulse of his life; and he purposefully sets forth to win her as his bride. He shrewdly encourages an enemy of his weakling uncle to murder the old man, after which he inherits what is left of the Delcasar money and property, a sum which still amounts to a good-sized fortune. His wealth creates in him a taste for tangible possessions: "the hunger for owning land, for dominating a part of the earth, was as much a part of him as his right hand" (115). He resolves to gain political control of a northern county, the location of much of the Delcasar land and the proposed route of a new railroad. In order to do so, he has to become a member of the *Penitentes*, a half-Christian, half-pagan cult that even today enjoys some prestige among the rural Mexican-Americans of New Mexico; the *Penitentes* practice self-flagellation and, during the Easter celebration, symbolically and sometimes actually crucify one of their number. Ramon undergoes the group's painful initiation rites and becomes a trusted *hermano* (brother). He then travels across the area "preaching the race issue" (125), and is somewhat surprised to find that he has great potential as a public speaker. The wretched peons and peasants listen breathlessly to his compelling, demagogic harangues. "Never once," Fergusson comments with deadly irony, "did he think of the incongruity of thus fanning the flames of race hatred for the love of a girl with grey eyes and yellow hair" (175).

Meanwhile, Julia continues to vacillate; she responds dutifully to the nearest and strongest influence. When she is with Ramon, she appears willing to do anything he wishes; when she is with her family, she seems reluctant even to see Ramon again. Finally, her relatives spirit her away to Europe, where she meets a young Anglo stockbroker whom she soon marries. Ramon is, of course, stricken; his elaborate plans shattered, he begins to question the validity of his feelings for Julia—to wonder if perhaps he loved her for what she represented to him, the shiny surface attraction of the Anglo's world, more than for what she really was. As the impulse of love wanes within him, the great energy that it sparked also begins to flag. He become apathetic, neglects the empire he had begun to build, and squanders his money on drink and poker. On several occasions Ramon's careless words echo with startling exactitude the indifference of his dissolute Uncle Diego. Playing the "gringo's" game, it seems, has been as disastrous for Ramon as it was for his immediate ancestors.

Ramon is briefly revived when he receives a letter from Julia, who is alone in New York while her husband is away on an extended business trip. He immediately catches a train for New York, and they enjoy a brief renewal of love. But Julia makes it plain that there will be no more such interludes, that she is finally and irrevocably married. Ramon, realizing now that there is not the slightest hope she will ever be his, numbly returns to the Southwest. On his arrival in New Mexico, he finds that the area is in the grip of a terrible drought and that the weather has decimated his lamb crop, which he had counted on to rebuild his dwindling finances. Demoralized, he sells all his holdings to

MacDougall, purchases a house for his mother in the fashionable section of town, and buys for himself a small irrigated farm a few miles upriver.

Ramon, who had always lived near the earth, passionately loves the mountains and desert of his home country. As a student in St. Louis, he had missed, not his family or town, but the lovely vistas of his native region. Now, weary of struggling, he surrenders to the soil and accepts as his own the life of a marginal farmer. That he is also in a sense retreating into the past is evidenced by the circumstance that the house on his farm is a crumbling hacienda, once the seat of a powerful and aristocratic family. Ramon is vaguely aware that to "trade his heritage for this was to trade hope and hazard for monotonous ease; but with the smell of the yielding earth in his nostrils, he no more thought of this than a man in love thinks of the long restraints and irks of marriage when the kiss of his woman is on his lips" (259). When last we see him, Ramon has taken a common-law wife, a Mexican-American girl who had come to the farm as a housemaid, and he has lapsed into an existence of indolence and sloth.

Within the framework of Fergusson's beliefs, as I have previously outlined them, there can be little doubt that Ramon is a failure. Certainly he cannot be scored for failing to become the grandee he once aspired to be, but he must be censured, the author implies, for his denial of destiny, for simply surrendering. Hints scattered throughout the book suggest that Ramon's true destiny lay in his undeveloped talents as an orator—that, had he been a stronger man, he might have become an effective champion of his people's rights and discovered in politics the fulfillment and power that he failed to find in love. In this sense, the stagnation of his abilities is not only a personal defeat but a tragic waste for the whole society, particularly for his Mexican-American brothers. Chronologically, *The Blood of the Conquerors* spans something less than two years; and the spectacular arc described by Ramon's rising and declining fortunes during that brief time is a striking illustration of a point the author makes in several of his books: as in the story of Catherine and Jim Royce, Fergusson seems to be saying, in his account of Ramon's disintegration, that romantic love is an extraordinarily flimsy and unreliable impulse by which to shape one's whole existence. And I believe that Fergusson is saying something else, something even more sweeping in its implications: that it is exceedingly difficult, if not impossible, for primitive or Medieval men to enter fully, in one generation, into the ranks of modern men.

In *Modern Man,* as we have seen, Fergusson divides the human race, according to its social and technological development, into three categories: primitive man; Medieval or Christian man; and modern man. In the Southwest, all three types of men are represented by various segments of the population. The Indian, to the degree that he still clings to his ancient tribal structure, is primitive man; the Spanish-American, especially if reared in the feudal atmosphere of a *rico* family, is Medieval man; and the Anglo, of course—the most recent addition to the scene—is modern man. Inexorably, the Anglo imposes his way of life upon the region. In a society run by machinery and dedicated to the making of money, men must have ready cash and must understand technology—conditions that work a hardship on most primitive or Medieval men. Those who possess money and technical expertise soon come to dominate those who do not. Ramon—who is of mixed Spanish and Indian blood and therefore justifiably represents both primitive and Medieval men—finds the Anglo's world attractive; but, because of his cultural and social heritage, he finds adjustment to it difficult. Indeed, his efforts to adjust prove in many ways disastrous.

Throughout the novel, much of Ramon's behavior is explained as having been motivated by his primitive nature. We are told, for example, that "He had the love of sensuous indolence, which, together with its usual complement, the capacity for brief but violent action, marked him as a primitive man—one whom the regular labors and restraints of civilization would never fit" (248). Like most primitive men, he believes in the workings of inscrutable fate; and, when his money begins to slip away from him, he becomes convinced that "bad luck had marked him for its prey" (253). Even his retirement to a small farm is attributed in part to a primitive desire to experience "the sweetness of being physically and emotionally at peace with the environment" (256). There is a brief but significant scene in the novel in which Ramon plays poker with Fitzhugh Chesterman, a "lunger" (a slang term, widespread in the Southwest, for a tubercular) from the East:

Never were the qualities of two races more strikingly contrasted. Ramon bluffed and plunged. Chesterman was caution itself, playing out antes in niggardly fashion until he had a hand which put the law of probabilities strongly on his side. Ramon was full of daring, intuition, imagination, bidding always for the favour of the fates, throwing logic to the winds. He was not above moving his seat or putting on his hat to change his luck. Chesterman smiled at these things. He was cold courage battling for a purpose and praying to no deities but Cause and Effect. (209)

Ramon's peculiarly difficult situation is that he finds himself cruelly suspended between two worlds, unable to partake fully of either. He elects, in order to win Julia, to pursue success according to the commercial values of the Anglo, yet he lacks the cultural equipment to do so. Once, traveling among the poor Mexican-Americans of a remote mountainous area, he is struck by the thought that "He was of their race and a growth of the same soil, but an alien civilization had touched him and sundered him from them, yet without taking him for its own" (165). It is hardly surprising that he is in some sense torn to pieces by opposing forces and is rendered incapable of sustained or purposeful action. Ramon, then, according to Fergusson's standards of conduct, fails; but the odds are from the beginning heavily against him. During most of the narrative he is struggling not only with the regressive psychological tendencies that all men at one time or another exhibit, but also, the author believes, with an anachronistic cultural heritage that in the modern world is an intolerable burden. For this reason perhaps, Fergusson appears to make at least an intellectual effort to understand Ramon (as opposed, for example, to his contemptuous dismissal of Jim Royce in *Women and Wives*); even so, the writer seems on occasion scarcely able to control his disgust at Ramon's betrayal of destiny. Lorene Pearson's claim that Fergusson's portrayal of Ramon is merely "intellection," that he achieves "no felt identity with Ramon" nor does he conduct any real search "into the psychology of the man," is unfortunately only too true.[8]

The Blood of the Conquerors is, nevertheless, a book with many virtues. Though Fergusson's first novel, it is written in the author's best and most graceful style, always one of the most attractive aspects of his works. From a sociological standpoint, it is a suggestive and still pertinent study of some of the problems that have tormented the Southwest for more than a century and no doubt will continue to do so in the future—the clash of cultures, for instance, and the ugly results of prejudice. In a way, the most striking effect of the novel, and of much of Fergusson's later fiction, is the ironic use it makes of the contradictory nature of the Southwest, of the fact that the region is both old and new: in a sense it has been civilized for hundreds of years; but, judged by the commercial standards of the Anglo, its development is recent and as yet incomplete. Old Town and New Town Albuquerque, allusions to which form a kind of *leitmotiv* in *The Blood of the Conquerors* and in several other of Fergusson's fictions, are fitting emblems of the conflict between the Old Southwest and the New, the primitive and the modern.

The novel's weaknesses, aside from those which derive from the author's ambiguous characterization of Ramon, have mostly to do with plot. The first half of the story is tightly and logically structured; but, in the second half, the narrative thread zigzags rather erratically; a number of incidents and details are included which, though interesting in themselves, appear to have slight relevance to the psychological crisis Ramon experiences. Moreover, the author, as in *Capitol Hill* and *Women and Wives*, seems a bit too insistent that his readers give unqualified assent to the premises on which he bases his characters' behavior. In this regard, he is not at all reticent about making categorical statements that seem at best debatable.

The following, for instance, is but one of many examples that might be cited of Fergusson's sweeping generalizations concerning the traits of Mexican-Americans: "Devotion to one particular bit of soil is a Mexican characteristic, and in Ramon it was highly developed because he had spent so much of his life close to the earth" (11). Several passages in the book begin, in effect, "Being Mexican, Ramon did such and such." Since Fergusson was not himself Mexican-American, he might well have exercised a more cautious restraint; the technique he employs—though certainly Fergusson does not carry it to such lengths—is, of course, the origin of many unpleasant ethnic stereotypes. In summation, *The Blood of the Conquerors* is a highly readable and thought-provoking work. But it is still a first novel, and is weakened by flaws that a more experienced writer might have avoided; therefore, it cannot, in my estimation, be placed in the front rank of the author's fiction.

III   *Flaming Youth in Albuquerque*

Hot Saturday, published in 1926, is the author's weakest and least-memorable novel. The story takes its name from the circumstance that the action occurs on a sweltering summer weekend; the title is also intended, no doubt, as a mildly salacious *double entendre*. The novel is laid in a Southwestern town—not identified but, as in *The Blood of the Conquerors*, obviously Albuquerque—in the 1920's; and the author, as always, makes good use of the more striking features of his regional setting. Indeed, the book's primary appeal to readers in the 1970's is as a detailed picture of early twentieth-century Albuquerque. As social history, the story derives its value from the assumption that Albuquerque was similar in many respects to dozens of other medium-sized towns of that period and that its history possesses, therefore, a measure of representative significance.

That this is a reasonable assumption Fergusson clearly demonstrates in *Hot Saturday* (and further documents in *Home in the West*, published two decades later). By the 1920's, the author writes, Albuquerque was already expanding "like a hardy weed that could grow anywhere and choke out any other growth."[9] Though only a few years removed from its frontier origins, the town is now run by bankers, lawyers, and real-estate agents; and it is no longer a hospitable home for the remaining old-timers who had helped to found it: "Pioneers did their job and gave way to money-makers in stiff collars and stiff respectabilities, cautious and over-disciplined as the pioneers had been wild and daring" (41). The town's young people seem uniformly restless and dissatisfied; their emotions are exacerbated, the writer claims, by the enticing possibilities of the automobile. The young share "a passionate love of motors and of fast and reckless driving. . . . cars had been excitement and escape. Cars had widened their lives, made many of the differences between them and the older generation they had to fight" (102).

Automobiles, in fact, have transformed the town and surrounding countryside, working a revolution that a few years before would have been unthinkable. Once awe-inspiring distances, for example, have been diminished severely:

Blatant flivvers loaded with giggling girls and smart young fellows in straw hats could make a trip in half an hour that would once have taken a good man all day. . . . Mountains that had been mystery and danger to one generation were a toy to the next. Pioneers had approached mountains with prayer, tightening their belts for want and effort, and their children flew up them and over them, spooned and feasted on their austere heights, found nothing there to harden body or spirit. . . . Mountains were no longer barrier nor adventure but they kept a certain dignity. The conquering town chucked them under the chin, threw trash in their faces, used them for playthings—but it could not use them for anything else. It could not plough them nor buy and sell them. (148–49)

Improved transportation has removed by the 1920's, the decade in which the novel is set, much of the town's isolated and ingrown character, and it now has a sizable representation of residents from other parts of the country. "Strangers who came to town," writes Fergusson, "were mostly of two kinds, commonly described as lungers and nuts" (125)—that is, health-seekers and artists. The former are welcomed because they boost the local economy; the latter are viewed with suspicion and distrust.

The central figure of *Hot Saturday,* the character through whose consciousness we see most of the action, is Ruth Bruck, who has matured in the midst of rapid change. Indulgence in automobiles, movies, and magazines has whetted her appetite for glamor and excitement; and her greatest desire is to escape the constraints of small-town life by migrating to the East. Her fantasies and dreams, consequently, are filled with images of escape and movement. Her father, Gus Bruck, is representative of a new kind of Southwesterner; for, after a rather reckless and misspent youth, he had developed an abiding faith in Albuquerque's future and had settled down to building a prosperous real-estate and insurance business. He had married a girl who was a pillar of propriety; but their only child, Ruth, twenty years old when the story occurs, despises her mother's strictures; and mother and daughter often quarrel bitterly. The two usually make up, however, with a torrent of tears; and on such occasions Ruth is overwhelmed by a child-like contrition. She sometimes escapes to the cellar beneath the Bruck home, her special place of refuge: "it had an attraction wholly indefinable. Going down into cool duskiness below the street was somehow comforting. It made her feel like a child again, sent her mind back to a time before her real battle had begun" (77). Despite this rather-too-obvious use of the cellar as surrogate womb (an example, incidentally, of the ill-digested Freudian theory that clots a great many novels published during the 1920's), the book's early chapters convincingly describe the barrier between generations that seems to have been greatly enlarged, if not erected, in twentieth-century America.

Though the events of the narrative occur during a single Au-

gust weekend, the previous twenty years of Ruth's life are high-
lighted in a series of flashbacks; and her relations with the men of
the town are a recurring subject of these glances into the past.
Very early, apparently, Ruth had acquired an unsavory reputation. Because she runs around with all kinds of men, she appears
to the town's more strait-laced citizens to be little more than a
tramp. To the men, she seems an unconscionable tease; she employs her generous physical endowments to arouse them, then
cruelly frustrates their desires. During the time immediately preceding the beginning of the novel, her two favorites have been
Conny Billop, a local ne'er-do-well, and John Romer, a handsome
"lunger" from the East. Romer, who in particular fascinates Ruth,
is a character cut from the mold of John Strome in *Women and
Wives*—calm, intelligent, self-assured, he always keeps his emotions in balance. Though he has little money, Ruth enjoys
Romer's company; and she is impressed by the fact that, unlike
most other men, he refuses to co-operate by playing her carefully
arranged games.

On the Saturday indicated in the novel's title, Ruth, despite
her affection for Romer, has contrived a daring plan to escape her
home town once and for all: she will seduce and marry Wilbur
Fadden, a visitor from the East and the heir to a shoe-polish fortune. She expects little trouble from Wilbur, who is gangling and
awkward; but she realizes that his domineering mother must be
circumvented by means of an immediate marriage. She invites
Wilbur to accompany the Bruck family on a picnic in the mountains, and there she maneuvers to get him alone by proposing
that they climb a nearby peak; by themselves she soon entices
him to kiss her, at first hesitantly, then passionately. After the
family's return to town, Ruth asks Wilbur to take her dancing at
the Willow Spring Pavilion, where bootleg liquor may be obtained. During the evening much dancing and drinking occurs,
and events become progressively livelier. Ruth is terrified when
several of her former suitors, including Romer and Conny Billop,
appear and begin whispering among themselves.

Desperate, she lures Wilbur to their car, where she artfully
suggests the possibility of their eloping. Wilbur, however, is a-
fraid of his mother's disapproval. When they re-enter the dance
hall, Conny manages to take Wilbur aside and apparently tells
him stories concerning Ruth's past behavior. Wilbur disappears,
and word arrives that he has called a taxi and returned home.

Ruth, angry and frustrated, begins crying. As "a slight anodyne for the sick disgust she felt" (241), she begins dancing with all who ask her; and the evening ends with Romer's taking her to his apartment, where now, beyond caring what happens, she goes to bed with him. The next morning, as Ruth sits on the front porch awaiting her family's return from church, she sees Wilbur ambling down the sidewalk. He awkwardly approaches and, to her astonishment, begins an anguished speech: "O Ruth! Can you forgive me for the way I acted last night? . . . Ruth, I need you! And I don't believe a word anyone says about you. . . . Ruth, I know you're good" (261).

The conclusion of *Hot Saturday*, needless to say, is tricky and unsatisfactory. The question of whether it was imposed honestly by the author or cynically by his editors is really beside the point: it bears an uncomfortable resemblance to the endings of formula stories usually found in slick magazines and, with its delicious irony, seems rather too neat to have occurred in any real-life situation. But the ending is only one of many esthetic difficulties that weaken the novel. Another is the plot which, as the foregoing discussion has no doubt suggested, is very slight and must support, somewhat creakily, the portentous weight of a succession of basically trivial events, Indeed, the tale related in *Hot Saturday* revolves around a single incident and seems little more than a prolonged short story. Though lengthy portions of the narrative are comprised of details concerning a variety of characters, none of the people in the book, with the partial exception of Ruth, comes alive as a living, breathing human being; most of them are simply caricatures who embody, in exaggerated form, defective character traits of one kind or another.

The novel, claims James K. Folsom, is "a chapter in Fergusson's own spiritual autobiography, a parable of his decision to move from the Southwest."[10] In a sense, Folsom is correct; the author's descriptions of Albuquerque and its citizens—the money-grubbing newcomers at least, as opposed to the pioneers—were obviously written with a pen dipped in acid. Since it is the story of a young woman trapped in the complacency, philistinism, and inflexible morality of the provincial middle class, *Hot Saturday* has inevitably been compared with Sinclair Lewis's *Main Street*.[11] Such a comparison, however, breaks down rather quickly since the only thing Lewis's and Fergusson's books have in common is a relentless hatred of and bitterness toward the impoverished conventions of small-town America; their methods of approaching their subjects differ considerably.

However, if Fergusson's primary aim in writing *Hot Saturday*, as Folsom's comment implies, was to plead with readers in 1926 to adopt his attitudes concerning middle-class values and to sympathize with the plight of the rebellious young—the self-styled "flaming youth" of the 1920's—who are fastened in the clammy grip of their elders (and it is entirely possible that this was indeed his major purpose), then he chose, in the character of Ruth Bruck, a singularly inappropriate vehicle by which to advance his convictions. Specifically, Ruth does not appear to be the kind of person who would benefit greatly from the change of environment she so ardently desires. Her behavior is often childish, and she is as full of illusions (acquired from early forms of the mass media, such as magazines and movies) as her mother is of pious platitudes. Perhaps in the future Ruth will develop a capacity for living life to the full—after her night with John Romer she awakens to a morning that seems "strangely new, clean and clear" (259)—but she lacks during most of the novel the emotional balance and self-awareness needed to exploit the freedom of movement and association afforded by a large city, her dreamed-of destination.

Moreover, while Ruth is plausible enough as a believable character type (her sexual teasing of men acquaintances, for instance, conforms to a fairly well-defined pattern of female behavior), her petulance and her petty cruelties scarcely enhance her credentials as a sacrificial lamb; as a symbol of suffering youth, she simply does not enlist the reader's sympathies. There is, of course, no inherent reason for criticizing the girl for failing to be a paragon of virtue; in fact, the mixture of personality traits ascribed to Ruth makes her, like Becky Sharp in Thackeray's *Vanity Fair*, a much more interesting and lively individual than the traditional virtuous heroine of the nineteenth- and early twentieth-century novel. The problem arises from the authorial comments in *Hot Saturday*, which seem to point to a sympathetic view of Ruth and her youthful colleagues. The inconsistency of these comments, when juxtaposed with Ruth's actual behavior, creates in the reader a good deal of confusion—confusion which fatally weakens an already shaky narrative.

Hot Saturday is an angry book. In it, to reiterate, the author mercilessly satirizes middle-class and small-town values. His satire is conveyed mainly through the attitudes of the various participants—the flatulent optimism of Gus Bruck, the saccharine piety of Mrs. Bruck, and the relentless rectitude that characterizes the public behavior of the town's leading citizens. Indeed, most of the people in the novel are portrayed as consenting victims of a monstrously rigid society; and, as such, they are objects of the writer's boundless contempt. They are made to seem almost unworthy of humane treatment; and this contempt is, I believe, the source of many of the novel's shortcomings. In dealing with contemporary matters about which he felt strongly, Fergusson apparently allowed his emotions—his anger and disgust in particular—to cloud his better judgment; his rage blinded him to the Brucks' humanity and blunted his artistic instincts. The unhappy consequence of the writer's emotional indulgence was a weak and unconvincing book, one marred by numerous esthetic lapses and one unredeemed by sympathy or tolerance for anyone other than Ruth.

CHAPTER 5

The Drifter

THE last of Fergusson's novels that have their settings in the twentieth-century Southwest are *Footloose McGarnigal* and *The Life of Riley*. The central characters of these two novels are alike in that each, during the course of the events chronicled, is a happy-go-lucky, amiable, and aimless man; each is a drifter in both a physical and moral sense; and each is a frustrated pioneer cast adrift in a world that seems to have closed its last frontier. But the two characters also differ in an important way: one of them, Alec McGarnigal, manages finally to right himself and to discover a new frontier in which his talents may be effectively utilized; the other, Morgan Riley, loses control of his life and eventually passes the chronological point of no return. Fergusson, as we have seen, believed that each person must diligently pursue his destiny and that, once revealed, destiny provides the individual with a conscious and directing purpose in life. Discovery and fulfillment of destiny, furthermore, require of an individual a large amount of concentrated effort, even hard work. In the author's philosophy, shiftlessness, whether intellectual or physical, is an unforgivable sin. In one sense, then, *Footloose McGarnigal* and *The Life of Riley* are fictional sermons which warn of the dire perils of drifting.

I A Wilderness Idyll

Readers of Fergusson's books are sometimes struck by the circumstance that there are very few characters in his fiction with whom the author seems personally to identify. One obvious exception to that general observation is Henry Lambert in *Capitol Hill*; another is Alec McGarnigal, the title character of *Footloose McGarnigal*, which was published in 1930. Certainly Alec's experiences, as detailed in the novel, closely parallel those of a specific phase of the author's career. On the basis of these parallels, I assume that Alec's odyssey in the mountains of New Mexico and his ultimate decision to return to the East are a fictional approximation of that period of the writer's life, between graduation from college and departure for a long residence in Washington, when he worked as a ranger in the Kit Carson National Forest.

Aside from *Home in the West*, *Footloose McGarnigal* appears to be Fergusson's only sustained attempt to take a long, hard look at his own personal experiences and their attendant moral and intellectual repercussions, and then to preserve his conclusions between hard covers. Admittedly, self-appraisal is a difficult task for anyone—absorbed, as most of us are, in the task of picking our way through the mine field of everyday necessities—and, if the effort, in this case, yielded at best mixed results, the novel that issued from it is nonetheless a courageous and interesting document.

As *Footloose McGarnigal* opens, it is spring, and Alec McGarnigal, who toils daily and anonymously in the office of a New York engineering firm, is troubled by a desire for "motion and change."[1] During this particular spring, Alec receives word that a Texas uncle, whose name is also Alec, has died and left his namesake a small sum of money. The young man, inspired by the example of his uncle's adventurous life, decides to use the money to abandon his job and wander wherever his inclinations lead him. Alec's uncle, it should be noted, is a recurring presence in the novel; but, having died before the story proper begins, he never appears as an actual character. As a child, Alec had listened with bug-eyed astonishment to his uncle's stories of the wild West; even as a college graduate in his mid-twenties, his imagination had been peopled with images drawn from those tales: Uncle Alec killing Indians and outlaws, Uncle Alec fighting off rustlers, Uncle Alec waving goodbye as he rides away from a weeping girl, and Uncle Alec as the central figure in a variety of romantic and improbable incidents. Indeed, Uncle Alec, according to the uncle's own testimony at least, had been one of the West's legendary characters; and his impressionable nephew vaguely yearns to follow in the older man's footsteps.

It seems, to anticipate a bit, that an important lesson of Alec's subsequent adventures—a lesson which of course is revealed to him only gradually—concerns the falsity of his uncle's reminiscences and the folly of any modern man's attempting to relive them. Uncle Alec's stories had been at once simplified and exaggerated, had consisted mainly of stereotyped characters and overblown incidents. The human participants in them, even Uncle Alec himself, it seems, had become little more than abstractions. Uncle Alec's tales, as a matter of fact, are very similar to those adventure stories of the West—"Westerns," as they are commonly called—that, since the Beadle Dime Novels of the nineteenth century, have been such an enduring and profitable aspect of the American publishing industry. In the actual world, Alec discovers, finding one's place and dealing with real people are a much more complex and tentative business than his uncle's bold narratives had suggested.

Alec, in any event, quits his job and heads for Texas. In San Antonio, he meets Syme, who is bound for New Mexico to assume command of a surveying crew sponsored by the Forest Service. Over a few drinks Syme offers Alec a minor position with his crew, and Alec eagerly accepts. In New Mexico, Alec becomes a timber cruiser; his job is to strike off into the mountains and estimate the board feet of timber on assigned plots of land. He quickly becomes accustomed to the mountain solitude and even enjoys the elemental existence imposed by the wilderness. After nightfall, the manly comradeship afforded by other members of the crew provides a measure of comfortable solace. He and his companions often talk long into the night, and predictably their talk is mostly about women. They had not "laid eyes on a woman for a month," the author writes; "but the longer they went without her in the flesh the more vividly she was present to their imaginations, demonstrating, as she always does, that to flee her is never to escape" (86).

In midsummer Alec decides that his best bet is to go to Taos and take an examination in hopes of becoming a full-time ranger with the Forest Service. Though he is reluctant to leave the natural beauty and good fellowship he has found in the mountains and among the crew, he departs with the expectation of soon returning. In Taos, he meets various representatives of the local artists' colony—"the most amazing collection of nuts in the world" (91), a friend tells him; and another acquaintance calls them exhibits in a "museum of misfits" (107). These episodes in Taos provide Fergusson an occasion to display his considerable talents as a satirist. The Taos artists are, as the author portrays them, mostly dilettantes and fakers, who are full of "sententious profundities" (136); even the serious ones are given to intellectual pretensions of the most contemptible sort.

Many of the artists, Alec discovers, have fastened on the Indians, whom they view as "noble savages," as worthy objects of their patronizing protection. There is, Alec muses, nothing censurable in aiding an oppressed minority—such assistance is indeed often a necessary and commendable labor—but many self-professed champions of the Indian, especially ones like the Taos intellectuals, are more interested in emotional compensations than in serious work on behalf of their supposed beneficiaries.[2] Alec, at any rate, is for a while amused by the spectacle he discovers in Taos. He is soon more disturbed than amused, however, for he begins to realize that the artists bear an unsettling, if somewhat remote, resemblance to himself: they are romantics searching in nature and in the primitive for something they believe they cannot find in the large cities of the East. Alec's most satisfying experience in Taos is his meeting and falling in love with Amaryllis Oldfield, a young sculptress who, like himself, is a temporary refugee from New York. Alec and Amaryllis go to a bizarre artists' party, attend the corn dance at Santo Domingo pueblo, and eventually sleep together. Amaryllis, however, disillusioned with her Taos colleagues, decides to return to New York; but Alec, for a time at least, must go back to the wilderness.

After passing the ranger's examination, Alec is assigned to a remote mountain station. His first duty is to man a fireguard until the end of a summer drought, after which he is given the job of patrolling on horseback adjoining government lands. It takes Alec only a few days once again to become accustomed to the rhythm of nature, and he is quickly content with this world of mountain glory. His solitary existence is disturbed, however, by the appearance of Lucretia Bullard, a girl from a nearby ranch. Lucretia and Alec begin riding together and are soon frolicking in mountain meadows. At first, Lucretia is merely a lovely diversion; but, when he learns that the girl feels trapped on the ranch and is desperately unhappy, he begins to pity her: "She had been at first a mystery to him and then a romantic challenge—a nymph on horseback, a vision of desire found in a forest. . . . Now for the first time he saw her as a real person in a real world. Her life was painfully clear to him—its meagerness, its pathetic alternatives" (254–55). Alec and Lucretia's affair ends abruptly when gossips in a nearby village inform one of the girl's male relatives of her amorous activities; the relative grimly warns Alec to stay away from her.

At this point, Alec is simply disgusted—with the people of the village, where personal privacy seems an inconceivable luxury, and with himself. He has not, he realizes, been a very diligent guardian of the public domain. He takes stock of himself and is not pleased by what he finds: he is wearing soiled and tattered clothing and a two-day growth of whiskers; and it "occurred to him, as a sudden surprising idea, that perhaps he was going to pot" (250). He immediately decides that he will return to the city—to "the monster he had fled" (273)—and find Amaryllis. He packs his gear, saddles his horse, and sets out for Taos. As he gallops through the night, his journey is interrupted by the sight of a transcontinental passenger train rushing out of the darkness: "In the dead blackness of the night it looked immensely alive, cutting the dark with swift fiery purpose, rushing unerringly through the black inhuman chaos of the mountain night toward great cities of light and order" (273). To Alec, the train is a reminder of the enticements and rewards of civilized society; and he is happy that he has discovered at last that the city is his true wilderness, "the frontier of his spirit" (274).

In his fascinating study *The Machine in the Garden*, Leo Marx isolates the locomotive as a characteristic and significant symbol in recent pastoral literature.[3] Since it represents the intrusion of civilization and technology into an idyllic pastoral setting, the train's connotations are usually elegiac and often highly unpleasant. In *Footloose McGarnigal*, however, Fergusson completely reverses these suggestive values. The pastoral retreat is dark and benighted, while the train symbolizes joy and light; Alec welcomes it as a good omen for the momentous personal decision he has just made. From this brief but important scene at the end of the novel, then, it is not difficult to formulate and extend the book's basic ideas. Edenic paradise, Fergusson implies, can be a peculiarly enervating and static environment. Nature is a lovely but dangerous refuge; its siren call is really an invitation to abdicate the responsibilities of civilized life. The pioneers, consequently, were not heroes to be emulated; they were often stunted creatures whose flight from society was a result of weakness; and the settlements they established on the fringes of the wilderness were ordinarily suspicious and inbred (like the village where Alec goes to buy supplies), as well as fearfully repressive.

Fergusson seems to assume also that the only link between many of these solitary frontiersmen and the amenities and comforts of society was woman; certainly, in *Footloose McGarnigal,* Alec is saved in large measure by the lure of Amaryllis, who has returned to the civilized East. There is an old saying that the frontier was "hell on horses and women," and the corollary to that truism is that women in primitive places, in order to lighten their terrible burden, usually attempt either to implant a new civilization or to return to the one they left behind. Western American literature is filled with female characters who are employed to represent civilized and social values and are therefore a check on the male's freedom of action (or, in Fergusson's terms, the man's tendency to regress to childish irresponsibility).

Fergusson—in *Footloose McGarnigal* and elsewhere in his fiction—accepts the female's symbolic role in the Western experience; but, as in his use of the locomotive, he reverses the symbol's usual connotations. Woman, he believes, rather than being just a threat to male freedom and autonomy, is a graceful emblem of life's finer possibilities. Unfortunately, in the writer's fiction she remains for the most part merely an emblem—a haunting, mysterious, and sometimes confusing image in the consciousness of his male characters—and she rarely develops into a believable human being. But this circumstance seems more a byproduct of American values and beliefs at the turn of the century (those outlined by Fergusson in *Home in the West)* than a personal failing on the part of the author.

Alec, at any rate, attempts for a time to re-enact the romantic roles his uncle's tales of the West had taught him. He becomes yet another manifestation of that stock figure in Western fiction—the lone drifter, fleeing the terrors of order and responsibility. But just as Fergusson, according to his account in *Home in the West,* never yielded completely to the temptation of wilderness solitude—"I always went back," he writes, "to my perspiring struggle, whether in Washington, New York, or Hollywood" (168)—so Alec recovers his sense of purpose in due time. We are encouraged to believe that, renewed by his wilderness idyl, he will return to city life and to Amaryllis with a great store of zest and energy. Within the context of the author's philosophy, the cautionary tale of Alec McGarnigal can have but one meaning: footloose drifting can be a useful restorative; but, prolonged for too lengthy a time, such shiftlessness becomes a regressive and destructive force, breaking down the drifter's sense of individuality.

Footloose McGarnigal is an important statement in that it provides a plausible philosophical explanation of why the writer found it desirable, even necessary, to leave his native region. Esthetically, however, the book is not wholly successful. As is true of several of the author's fictions, the novel is marred by a rather aimless plot. Fergusson too often yields to the temptation to include interesting but essentially irrelevant descriptions and details; sometimes potential incidents are begun only to be abruptly dropped. The book might well have been titled *The Adventures of Footloose McGarnigal* since it is comprised of a series of episodes not always causally connected. But they *are* usually connected thematically, since all are intended to illustrate the unstated propositions outlined above. For this reason, the novel is a more coherent and effective work than, say, *Capitol Hill,* the sprawling structure of which seems almost totally shapeless. Despite flaws, *Footloose McGarnigal* has its strengths, and it may well be, as several critics have claimed,[4] the best of Fergusson's novels set in the twentieth-century Southwest. Its tone is light, almost deprecating, an effect which is on the whole pleasing. And, while its incidents often seem trivial, they are deceptively so; when probed, they sometimes yield rich and provocative meanings.

II   *The Life of a Failure*

Fergusson's final attempt to portray the contemporary Southwest in fiction was *The Life of Riley,* which appeared in 1937.

The novel is a chronicle history of the life and times of Morgan Riley from his birth around the turn of the century to a restless middle age during the Depression of the 1930's. Essentially it is the account of a series of sexual encounters, for Riley's sole proficiency and almost his only interest is the seduction of women. The first chapter gives details of the hero's ancestry. His father, Jim Riley, is a successful Albuquerque saloonkeeper; and his mother, a frail Southern girl, dies soon after Morgan is born. Riley's father allows the boy, during his early years, to do very much as he pleases; and his freedom, combined with his exceptional athletic skills in such games as football and tennis, lends Morgan considerable influence on his youthful peers. He becomes the leader of a gang notorious for its imaginative pranks. Riley also develops an early curiosity about girls, though the Anglo mothers' close supervision of their daughters usually frustrates his planned experiments. His sexual initiation, in his midteens, is effected through the agency of a Mexican-American girl named Consuelo.

Riley's first real passion occurs in late adolescence when he falls in love with Anne Bledsoe, whose socially conscious mother is grimly opposed to her daughter's marrying the son of an Irish saloon owner. Anne and Riley's clandestine affair is intense and satisfying, but it is terminated when Anne finally decides to go East to pursue her destiny as a painter. Riley, disappointed by her decision and somewhat at loose ends, resolves to enlist in the United States Army, which is about to embark on the great adventure of World War I. In Europe, Riley, accustomed by his training in sports to short bursts of energy and concentration, easily distinguishes himself on the field of battle. After about a year, however, he receives word of his father's death, news which provokes in him feelings of deep nostalgia. Jim Riley had once been a wealthy man, but at his demise he retained only a combination pool room and cigar store, called the Lucky Spot, to bequeath to his son. Riley nonetheless decides that he will go back after the war to his home town and run his father's small enterprise.

Back in Albuquerque, Riley is for a time thoroughly disoriented. Adolescence and young manhood, writes Fergusson, are "a miserable prelude to living for some and for others a romantic experience never to be transcended."[5] For Riley they are obviously the latter. Following the satisfactions of being a sports and war hero, everything in mature life appears anti-climactic; adult-hood seems to offer no possibility for growth. Though his store quickly becomes a favorite gathering place for the town's male population, Riley inherits his father's rather disreputable social standing; and he is shunned by his friends' wives. He has an op-portunity, but refuses, to gain a foothold in Albuquerque's busi-ness community. Instead, he spends his days among the pool-room idlers, taking time off for frequent hunting trips.

Eventually Riley is reunited with a childhood playmate named Lillian Kringle. Lillian is something of a shrinking violet, and she arouses Riley's protective instincts. They are soon married, and for a time are comfortably happy. Then Riley's thirst for fresh ad-venture leads him into an involvement with a beautiful young widow. Inevitably, Lillian discovers his infidelity and seeks refuge with her family, now living in El Paso. Riley, motivated partly by pride and partly by apathy, declines to follow her with hat in hand.

Years pass, and various women enter Riley's life only to exit shortly thereafter. The Great Depression begins, and he contracts numerous debts to keep his store in operation. Clarence Weston, a wealthy Easterner, buys into the business and soon owns a con-trolling interest. Clarence is little more than a spoiled child; he is unattractive but has a taste for nice-looking girls. At first, Riley pities him and makes dates for him. Clarence, however, once he assumes command as Riley's boss, becomes even more demand-ing; he makes Riley, in effect, his personal procurer. Riley natur-ally finds this occupation distasteful, but he uncomplainingly fills his appointed role. One day, as Riley is feeling the weight of ap-proaching middle age, he picks up outside town a penniless hitchhiker, a young ranch girl named Shirley Skeen, who has run away from home. He helps her find a cheap room and a job in a local department store, and Shirley is appropriately grateful. Her youth and beauty stir Riley's blood as no woman has in years, and she in turn seems pleased with his expert love-making.

Presently, however, Shirley obtains a better job in El Paso, and Riley begins driving there to see her on weekends. In a Juarez nightclub one evening, they are accosted by a boy from Shirley's home town who has been frantically searching for her. As the two young people dance, Riley admits a painful truth to himself: despite Shirley's gratitude, she does not really love him.

He slips quietly out of the club and returns to his hotel, where he disgustedly takes stock of his life and even contemplates suicide. For years, he realizes, he has been steadily declining—"a degeneration so gradual he had never before been aware of it. As a youth he had been a great success, as a man he had simply found nothing to do" (314). Now, growing old alone and in financial bondage to another man, life seems hardly worth continuing.

But, instead of pulling the trigger of the gun he buys, he decides on an impulse to call Lillian, who works as a stenographer for an El Paso business firm. At first, Lillian is surprised and rather cool; and he is dismayed to find that she has developed into an independent and self-assured woman. It soon becomes apparent, however, that she is happy to see him, indeed still loves him; and at novel's end a reconciliation seems imminent. At this point, the reader is reminded of an authorial comment from earlier in the novel: most men, Fergusson says, begin "by trying to keep themselves free of feminine domination and most ended, as they had begun, by hanging onto a skirt" (189–90). As Riley's powers have diminished, Lillian's have grown; and now she is the stronger of the two. Riley ridicules himself for ever having thought of suicide. His seeing Lillian again puts him in a mellow frame of mind, and he decides that he must finally adjust himself to life's uneventful flow and accept the certainty of physical decay. "His life," he reflects at novel's end, "was not a passion or a tragedy after all. It was just a compromise. . . . He was a failure and for reasons beyond his knowing. He accepted the fact, a little sadly, but without bitterness. He was no more capable of tragedy than he was capable of success" (327).

Structurally, *The Life of Riley* is a chaotic and confusing work. There are lengthy time lapses between chapters, as well as abrupt shifts of narrative focus. Detailed life histories are provided for most characters, even minor ones; sometimes a participant's parentage, birth, childhood, and adult career are traced only to have the character precipitately dropped from the storyline. Many episodes in the novel seem separable units, which, if lifted from the book, would scarcely be missed. In the first chapter, for example, Fergusson describes Riley's father and mother, their reasons for migrating to Albuquerque, and their unlikely courtship: Riley is mentioned only as an unnamed baby—the product of their union. This segment could easily be detached from the narrative and printed as a short story (in fact, it is possible that it was first written as such). With many bumps and jolts—and occasional intervening passages which are serene, even dull enough to put the reader to sleep—the book jogs along to its muted conclusion. It is, in short, fully as loose and disjointed as *Capitol Hill*. Indeed, in the final accounting, *The Life of Riley* must be lumped with *Capitol Hill* and *Hot Saturday* as the least successful of the author's novels.

But, despite its flaws, *The Life of Riley* is not without interest, especially if it is viewed in the context of Fergusson's other writings. For one thing, the novel appeared in 1937, a year after the publication of *Modern Man*. It is reasonable to assume, I think, that there was a degree of overlapping in the composition of the two books and that the beliefs and areas of concern developed in *Modern Man* were much on the author's mind as he wrote *The Life of Riley*. The career of Morgan Riley, in fact, seems almost a laboratory experiment in how to *avoid* becoming a "modern man." Like Ramon Delcasar in *The Blood of the Conquerors*, Riley is essentially primitive and therefore is incapable of living successfully in the modern world. "He had little patience," the writer tells us, "no industry, no special ambition, but he had a considerable capacity to meet emergency. It was only in moments of great excitement that he felt his power . . ." (102).

Riley, a rather pitiful drifter, floats through a society in which drifting ordinarily ends in shipwreck. He has no ability for sustained labor, none of the plodding hopes for deferred rewards that contemporary life requires. His potential as a businessman is nil. His contacts with other people, furthermore, are initiated almost wholly on the basis of sentimentality—according to Fergusson, a dangerous and usually spurious emotion; his pity for Clarence Weston, for example, leads to a degrading partnership. Riley possesses hardly any internal equilibrium, and indeed "Inner conflict left him helpless . . ." (116). He usually escapes his problems by going hunting. Sometimes he seeks refuge in the past, for he is a man much given to nostalgia, and often for hours at a stretch he daydreams about past glories.

Even in his relations with women—the most successful phase of his life—Riley is in some ways a failure. In his fiction Fergusson usually portrays the relationship between a man and a woman as being, of necessity, that of adversaries; male and female often

complement and fulfill each other, but basically they work at
cross purposes; but Riley, suffused with sentiment, cannot accept
such a detached appraisal. His mind sometimes plays over the
vast superstitious lore that has attempted to explain woman's
mysterious motives and behavior, and he tries to arrive at a systematic theory of seduction. Essentially, however, his approach is
intuitive, and his ability to please is simply a natural gift. He accepts that gift hungrily, and he exercises his power over women
with reckless abandon; in Riley, as one critic has perceptively observed, "the lone hunter of frontier days becomes the wolf of the
twenties and thirties."[6]

At times, however, Riley insists on burdening a purely physical
arrangement with the excess baggage of emotion. In the midst of
an affair, for example, he occasionally conjures up the image of
Anne Bledsoe, his ideal of the perfect lover. He often thinks guiltily of his treatment of Lillian, though their separation, as he later
finds, was the best thing that could have happened to her since it
allowed her to become a confident and self-sufficient individual.
His infatuation with Shirley Skeen is in part the result of pity and
a recurrent instinct to protect the helpless. Thus preoccupied,
Riley sees his life slipping away from him, admits that he is "a
failure and for reasons beyond his knowing" (327).

The serenity with which he finally concedes this last point is
derived in large measure from the social and economic problems
that surround him: as he looks at his fellows, he sees very few
who are *not* failures. Indeed, national economic conditions provide throughout the novel a subtle parallel to the fluctuations in
Riley's personal fortunes. His own flush times, World War I and
the years immediately following, are a period of growing prosperity for the nation; his sinking to the nadir of contemplated suicide
is appropriately played out against the backdrop of the Great Depression.

I have no proof to support my contention, but it seems to me
that Fergusson, in the character of Morgan Riley, is deftly satiriz-
ing the typical Hemingway hero, a figure much in the thoughts of
literary men in the 1930's. Like the main (male) character of a
Hemingway story or novel, Riley is "an expert in war and sport
and women" (109). Even as the world disintegrates around him,
Riley clings to a semblance of order by exercising his craftsmanship in the performance of some trivial task; at crucial moments

in his life, for instance, he ordinarily goes hunting, thereby simultaneously evading his problems and shoring up his ego through the demonstration of his superlative skills as a hunter. He is a man of action, not of reflection; he lives for the moment, for those experiences of intense pleasure and excitement in which he may prove himself as a man.

The difference between Hemingway and Fergusson is that the latter writer follows his creation far beyond the gratifications of the moment, and thus uncovers the Hemingway hero's fatal flaw: he simply has no capacity for enduring the murderous grind of everyday routine. Just as the reader cannot conceive a Hemingway character as settling down to a normal job and as rearing a family, neither can he envision Riley's following such a course. Though the ending of the novel seems hopeful, the people in the book will not necessarily live "happily ever after"; the future for Riley, even in middle age, remains problematical.

Despite many technical difficulties, therefore, *The Life of Riley* contains a number of interesting elements which are well worth the reader's close scrutiny. Another such element in the book is the occasional passage in which Fergusson demonstrates his truly remarkable talent for discerning the underlying pattern of a given social situation. Several examples might be cited, but an especially good one is the lengthy description of the males who regularly assemble at Riley's establishment, the Lucky Spot. Most of the men, the author tells us, "were sportsmen of a certain standing and most of them had some gift as story-tellers. This was, in its way, a literary circle. None of its members ever thought of it as such but a certain kind of unwritten folklore was here diligently gathered, exploited, perfected and criticized" (205–06). As the passage continues, it becomes increasingly resonant of echoes from the racial past. It is, the reader realizes, not just the depiction of a group of modern dandies but a scene at least as venerable as the human race itself: tribal hunters surrounding a campfire are entertained by the recitations of bards. Many of Fergusson's portraits of contemporary society possess this stunning quality of timeless depth; in them, the immediacy of the moment is set within a context of customs that are generations —perhaps centuries—old.

But, while the text of *The Life of Riley* sometimes glitters with such unexpected jewels, it is for the most part dismally disap-

pointing. Certainly, it does not measure up in overall effectiveness to *The Blood of the Conquerors* or to *Footloose McGarnigal*,
the best of the writer's novels set in the twentieth-century
Southwest (and even they, as I have shown, are weakened by
serious flaws). Distressed no doubt at his inability to come to
grips with modern life in his fiction, Fergusson, after publishing
The Life of Riley, abandoned the writing of novels for almost a
decade and a half. When he returned to fiction in 1950, with the
appearance of *Grant of Kingdom*, he seems tacitly to have admitted that the permanence of history perhaps offers a form and
perspective not afforded by the amorphous present. This admission, whether or not consciously made, proved a boon not only to
the author but to the whole of American literature.

CHAPTER 6

Southwestern History: The Dynamics of Change

THE pervading weakness of Fergusson's fictional studies of the twentieth-century Southwest—aside from those difficulties with characterization and plotting which frequently recur—is the author's eagerness to serve as his characters' judge, jury, and executioner, rather than as merely the dispassionate observer. The writer seems to have too many axes to grind, too many preconceptions about what he believes is the inevitable direction of human behavior, and, to make matters worse, too marked an inclination to indulge in facile exposition of those preconceptions. Though the force of his narrative talents sometimes enables his books to overcome, if not eliminate, these difficulties, the results of his preconceptions are often incidents which appear contrived and characters who seem little more than puppets who are ruthlessly condemned to act out their creator's carefully patterned scenarios. In short, the presence in the narratives of the author and of his inflexible principles of behavior is too strongly felt; as a consequence, Fergusson's novels laid in the modern West fail, on the whole, to generate that illusion of objectivity and spontaneity that is a feature of most good storytelling.

The ripest fruits of the writer's considerable abilities, I believe, are his four fictions set in the nineteenth-century Southwest—*Wolf Song, In Those Days, Grant of Kingdom,* and *The Conquest of Don Pedro*—and his work of local history, *Rio Grande.* Fergusson admitted, in various sources, to being ineluctably drawn to the region's colorful history, while at the same time viewing that history with a detached and suspicious eye; an interest in the past, after all, betrays regressive psychological tendencies, and any retreat into the static structure of historical events, Fergusson contended, is simply a form of escape from the present. Still, the gulf of years between past and present seemed to impose on the writer's imagination a useful discipline, and in the best of his historical fiction he managed to avoid most of those problems that beset his works laid in more recent times. He was sympathetic, even romantic, in his approach to the past; but, in portraying his pioneering forebears, he nonetheless clung steadfastly to his relentlessly honest, if arguable, theory of human behavior. The result (in such books as *Grant of Kingdom* and *The Conquest of Don Pedro*) is a supremely convincing synthesis of character, landscape, and historical moment—a synthesis which somehow bespeaks both objective detachment and sympathetic understanding.

Fergusson apparently saw the West's history as a great drama of endless change, and the fortunes of individuals and institutions as the outgrowth of their ability, or inability, to adjust to change. But this concept is only an informing principle, which serves as the substructure for a variety of technical approaches. Concerning his specific methods of employing the West's frontier past, the writer provided an interesting and valuable statement in the introduction to *Followers of the Sun: A Trilogy of the Santa Fe Trail* (1936)—a volume which brings together three of his fictions: *The Blood of the Conquerors, Wolf Song,* and *In Those Days.* "I approached the past first," he writes, "with a romantic impulse—a wish to create a world out of my own longing . . ."[1] As he grew older, he gradually suppressed the desire to use his creative imagination as a means of escaping to the past; he came to understand that romantic misfits—who, like Minniver Cheevy, think they have been born too late—only cheapen and destroy history. He also came to see that those who look to the future, as Fergusson (writing in the mid-1930's) claims he now does, do not necessarily disregard history; for history has much to teach the observant individual concerning the course of human affairs. If one understands the reality of the past, then he better comprehends the present that the past has created; and in the Southwest, the writer asserts, this is doubly true since past and present in that region are separated, at most, by only a few decades.

Fergusson concedes that the traditional portrayal of the Western experience in fiction, from Beadle Dime Novels to modern-day "Westerns," has been weak and inadequate. Most critics attribute these books' shortcomings to the widespread use of melodramatic plots by writers of Western romances; the author, however, believes that these weaknesses are primarily the result of lifeless and unrealistic characters. Melodrama was in reality an authentic element of the pioneers' experience; for some, it was a part of their everyday life. Western fiction, then, is not essentially unrealistic in its typical plot formulas: "Its stories are taken from the life, but its people from the literary past. They are all, or nearly all, sired by Sir Walter Scott and damned by the Genteel Tradition."[2]

Ideally, then, Fergusson's approach to Western history is through the portrayal of believable human characters—and, incidentally, through a restrained use of dramatic incident. Though he asserts that melodrama within a frontier context is a defensible literary tool, he certainly does not employ sensational events in the degree or variety that most Western writers do. "The proper business of a novelist, as I conceive it," Fergusson says, "is to reduce themes of social significance to terms of individual destiny and so to give them life."[3] The author believes that the principles of human behavior—people's motives, appetites, and relationships with their fellows—remain basically the same in any period; and a change of locale or historical date does not remove the writer's responsibility to describe that behavior realistically. He concludes, therefore, that a more faithful adherence to these principles of behavior should erase the "romantic" label that is ordinarily attached to any novel set in the nineteenth-century West.

I   *The Great River and Its History*

Anyone who has been reared in the Southwest—especially someone like Fergusson, who grew up in New Mexico around the turn of the century—can scarcely remain unaware of the region's fascinating past. During his childhood, the author says in *Home in the West,* "the country around Albuquerque was a living museum of its own history . . . Schoolbook history I found a bore but the history of my region became as real to me as my own experience" (12). Tales told by old-timers had the immediacy of a wilderness that could still be glimpsed in the mountains and desert that surround his home town; they engendered in the boy that early romantic attitude toward the past which he alludes to in the introduction to *Followers of the Sun*. Many of his hunting forays indeed were conducted as "a kind of play-pioneering," as an attempt to recreate a still vividly remembered history. "I do not wish to romanticize myself as a youth on horseback," he writes, "or to entertain the reader with any account of my adolescent exploits. . . . What seems to me relevant to my work is that I did passionately long to relive the past. . . ."[4]

When he was a young reporter in Washington, as I have indicated, Fergusson often drew upon the resources of the Library of Congress; nostalgic for his native region, he read widely in the library's collection of Western Americana—reading that proved invaluable in his later career as a novelist. To those familiar with the literary record of the nineteenth-century West, that record seems scarcely "literary" at all. It is mostly a series of historical documents—first-person accounts of exploration and adventure, eye-witness descriptions of colorful people and events—which possess, in varying degrees, literary value. Though the bulk of this material is simply a tedious chronicle of the pioneers' everyday life and experiences, anyone wishing to deal with the history of the West, whether in an imaginative or scholarly fashion, must be intimately familiar with such writings.

And in this regard, certainly, Fergusson conscientiously did his homework. He even helped add to the available stock of these primary materials. In 1930 he wrote the introduction to *The Last Rustler: The Autobiography of Lee Sage* and was apparently instrumental in getting the book published. Fergusson says he first met Lee Sage in Salt Lake City in 1927. Impressed by Sage's talent as a teller of tales, he encouraged the older man to write down his reminiscenses; then Fergusson tailored the manuscript for publication. Most memoirs by old-timers, Fergusson contends, "are bald outlines of events, lacking the observation of detail and the power of imagination that it takes to make a narrative live."[5] Sage's autobiography, Fergusson believes, is one of the best of Western memoirs. *The Last Rustler*, it is interesting to note, is dedicated to Fergusson: "an artist-lover of distant horizons and the lure of unmarked trails."[6]

One of the most attractive and useful products of the author's broad knowledge of Western Americana is *Rio Grande,* a kaleidoscopic history of northern New Mexico, first published in 1933. For the beginning student of Southwestern history, the bibliographical note which Fergusson appends to his text is a kind of basic library of primary source materials that concern the region's nineteenth-century past. The writer acknowledges his indebtedness to George W. Kendall's *Narrative of the Texan-Santa Fe Expedition,* to Josiah Gregg's *Commerce of the Prairies,* to George Frederick Ruxton's *Life in the Far West,* to W. W. H. Davis's *El Gringo,* to J. R. Bartlett's *Personal Narrative,* to William French's *Recollections of a Western Ranchman,* and to numerous other similarly important works of the kind.

Taken together, these classic accounts of the nineteenth-century Southwest supply firsthand descriptions of virtually every character type who inhabited the region in those days: mountain men and Indians, Spanish aristocrats and freighters from the Santa Fe Trail, cowboys and cavalrymen, hunted outlaws and "greenhorns" from the East. But such accounts, even those which attain a high level of perception and style, are merely the raw materials of history and art: it remains for the imaginative writer to synthesize the facts they provide in a powerful and living narrative. This Fergusson does, with memorable results, in *Rio Grande.*

The book takes its title, of course, from one of the Southwest's great water courses. The narrative focuses, however, not on the river's entire length, but on its two-hundred-mile flow from the Colorado border to Albuquerque. The life that exists between these two points is demonstrably supported by the river's precious water; and, within the area it drains, an astonishing variety of human experience and social forms has occurred over the years. Fergusson not only read about the history of this region; during his lifetime, he carefully explored every part of its topography, from the floor of the river valley to the summit of Wheeler Peak near Taos, more than thirteen thousand feet above sea level. The Rio Grande, according to his sister Erna, is a "river he has swum in, hunted along, jumped when it was low, fought when it was high."[7] He had an opportunity to observe for himself the life-giving properties of its muddy water, with the result that, as Lawrence Clark Powell has said, his books about northern New Mexico "smell of river-bottom and pine-forest, not of library stacks. . . ."⁸ In *Rio Grande* personal experience, diligent research, and the author's gifts as a prose stylist are brought into perfect register, and the resultant blend more than meets J. Frank Dobie's definition of good historical writing: "when interpretative power, just evaluation, controlled imagination and craftsmanship are added to mastery of facts."⁹

The organization of the book conforms to that three-part scheme of mankind's historical development that the writer sets forth in *Modern Man:* primitive man, followed by Medieval or Christian man, who in turn is followed by modern man. In *Rio Grande,* Fergusson describes first the Southwest's pre-Columbian inhabitants, the Indians; next, he chronicles the arrival, in all their feudal splendor, of the Spanish; and he closes with the nineteenth-century intrusion of the Anglos. The region's history, he says in the work's introduction, "describes the aboriginal America which is typical of all primitive life. It recounts the last aggressive thrust of religious empire on this continent and the decay of a lost and isolated fragment of that world. It pictures the modern man in the sharp contrast of conflict with these older cultures, first as a fighting hunter, then as a trader and explorer and finally as the master and slave of his machines."¹⁰ The Southwest, Fergusson believes, is a land peculiarly well suited to display the flow of history. In an arid, rocky country change does not come quickly; and, when it does come, vestiges of the past are slow to disappear; centuries-old artifacts are easily preserved in the dry air of New Mexico. The climate also seems to harden and preserve modes of human life, for unlike most sections of the United States, the region's present population still contains large numbers of historical throwbacks.

In the book's first chapter, "The Dancing Builders," the author describes the efforts of the Pueblo Indians to establish a perfectly harmonious and cooperative community, an effort that was not altogether successful, but one which continues even in the middle of the twentieth century. In the American Indian, Fergusson writes,

as in all primitives, individual personality does not exist as it does in civilized men. The Indian is not the free being of romantic legend. On the contrary, almost everything he does and everything he believes is dictated by tradition. He is surrounded by social taboos and compulsions and more completely controlled by them than is even the most conventional of civilized men. The individual part of him is small and weak, the communal and traditional part massive and rigid. The Indians produce few great leaders in any line because greatness is individual. Indian leaders for the most part are figureheads who merely repeat traditional words and acts. (59–60)

Though greatly diminished in number, Indians persist in the Southwest, but they no longer rule. They relinquished their dominance, the author insists, because their society failed to cultivate effective leadership. They never reached "the point, in man's long ascent toward consciousness, at which great leaders are produced" (60).

The Spanish explorers who came to the Southwest, beginning in the sixteenth century, were men "governed by a double authority, that of God and that of Empire" (47). They and their followers established in the region a feudal society of microcosmic grandeur. It was an enclosed world ruled by men who were "proud and lazy and often . . . cruel but the society they created had charm because it was imbued with respect for the past. . . . Perhaps the aristocratic ideal was never more completely realized, on a small scale and in a rude way, than it was along the Rio Grande. . . ." (77–78). The Spanish aristocrats called themselves *gente de razon* (the right people), or *ricos* (rich ones). They ruled in a grand and despotic style, controlling absolutely their land and the people attached to it—especially the wretched peons (equivalents of European serfs) and the Spanish women, who were rigidly and jealously guarded.

Their society, governed wholly by the exigencies of caste and custom, was presided over by an institution that zealously promoted those customs: the Church. Fergusson believes that a significant feature of Medieval man's philosophy and behavior is the circumstance that he is thoroughly Christian. Explorers and *conquistadores* who entered the Southwest were accompanied by priests, whose high (if unattainable) goal was to convert the new-world natives. The *ricos,* if they feared anyone, feared and respected God's representatives in their communities, granting them generous prerogatives. In the mountains, the *penitente* brothers, partly a religious cult and partly a social and political organization, were secretly encouraged and directed by the rural priests. As a symbol of the Church's privileged status in Spanish New Mexico, the author isolates and describes at length Padre

Martinez of Taos. Martinez enthusiastically promoted the Church's influence on the population, while at the same time amassing considerable personal power, even to the extent of openly maintaining a harem of pretty girls. To Fergusson, Martinez is an emblem of Medieval Catholicism's mediating and compromising role in bridging the gap between primitive communitarianism and modern individualism. In this regard, incidentally, the reader should compare Fergusson's generally sympathetic description of Martinez with Willa Cather's hostile portrait in *Death Comes for the Archbishop*.

But, if the old world was "a jackass ridden by a priest, the new one was a jackass ridden by a lawyer" (225). And from the Anglos' first tentative contacts with the area, it seemed inevitable that they, bearers of an expansive and money-oriented social ethic, would some day dominate New Mexico's ancient and blood-stained soil. The first Anglos in the region, however, though they may have been a tiny wave of the future, must have looked very much like relics of a savage past. They were called "mountain men," and they were barbaric renegades bent on adventure and on the accumulation of treasure in the form of beaver pelts. These emissaries of "civilization" were soon followed by troopers of the conquering United States Army, traders funneled into the area by the Santa Fe Trail, cowboys and ranchers spilling over from the cattle culture of neighboring Texas, and finally all the assorted middle-men of commerce that were brought in by the railroads.

In particular, the Santa Fe Trail, a meandering artery of trade beginning at Independence, Missouri, and ending in northern New Mexico, seemed to inhabit the author's imagination with a special vividness. His own past was linked to the Trail, since his maternal grandfather came to New Mexico by means of it, and he often alludes to it in his writings. It appears to represent for Fergusson the first inefficient but portentous intrusion of modern American commercialism into what was essentially a primitive and Medieval culture. In *Rio Grande*, the writer devotes an entire chapter to Josiah Gregg, himself a freighter and author of *Commerce of the Prairies*, a classic account of the Trail's heyday. Fergusson apparently saw in Gregg a kindred spirit, a man who spent his life alternately yielding to the impulse to acknowledge his social responsibilities on the one hand and on the other to the impulse which sprang from the lure of the open prairies. But Gregg, as he is described in *Rio Grande*, is more than just a prototype of the author. With him, Fergusson believes, "the modern spirit went into the wilderness, undaunted and uncorrupted, perhaps for the first time" (173).

The true vehicle of "the modern spirit," however, was not the freight wagon but the railroad. "The Rio Grande valley," the writer says, "had suffered many powerful invaders but the one with the belly that ate coal and wood, the eye that bored a hole in the dark, the voice that shouted across the miles, made all the others seem puny. All previous invaders the country had absorbed. . . . This one created a world of its own—a world of iron, work and money" (272–73). The railroad, truly "the machine in the garden," changed forever what had been, even in the late nineteenth century, a pastoral, easy-going society. In Albuquerque, it gave rise to a settlement of wooden stores, office buildings, and shabby residences that came to be known as New Town—the fortress of Anglo money and business. Meanwhile Old Town, built mainly of adobe and attuned to a more relaxed tempo, continued to exist very much as it always had—the visible symbol of an ancient, threatened way of life. Though Fergusson terminates his account of New Mexico's history at this point—that is, near the beginning of the twentieth century—it is clear that the coming of the railroad initiated a trend that succeeding decades have served only to expand and intensify.

If the materials in *Rio Grande* are structured around a single paraphrasable theme, that theme seems best summed up in the following statement: "The character of a country is the destiny of its people . . ." (9). A land as harsh and demanding as northern New Mexico inevitably plays a part in shaping the lives of its inhabitants. Probably Fergusson is saying here much the same thing as Ross Calvin says in *Sky Determines*, an evocatively titled study of the Southwest: "In New Mexico," writes Calvin, "whatever is both old and peculiar appears upon examination to have a connection with arid climate. Peculiarities range from the striking adaptation of the flora onwards to those of the fauna, and on up to those of the human animal."[11] The Southwest attracts certain kinds of people (and animals) and repels others; those who remain must adapt themselves to its special ways and are irrevocably altered in the process. Even the money-culture of the Anglo, in the face of impenetrable necessity, has subtly adjusted to the region's unique conditions. Change will and must occur, but land and sky endure; they resist only those who fail to acknowledge their awesome, inert power.

In *Modern Man,* as I have previously shown, the author clearly favors the era of the modern. In *Rio Grande,* his sympathies seem divided; each of the three cultures he describes has its strengths and weaknesses. Societies and institutions, Fergusson suggests, falter and decay when they do not foresee and allow for changing conditions; but their myopia, he implies, is not necessarily censurable since it may be simply a matter of the completion of a life cycle: when energy is spent and the will to live dissipated, there is little reason to continue existing. Fergusson's ambivalence in this regard, however, does not dilute his book's effectiveness; paradoxically, the sense of ambivalence greatly enhances the work's power. *Rio Grande* possesses an objectivity and authority that *Modern Man* aspires to achieve but never attains. Perhaps the modest goal of the former work—chronicling the past of one relatively small region rather than trying to account for the whole of human history and culture—explains its manifest superiority over the latter. Perhaps also the author's intimate familiarity with his subject is the source of his tentative attitude in the former, for it is ordinarily true that the more one knows about a segment of history, the less categorical are his generalizations about it.

Certainly *Rio Grande* springs from vast knowledge and research. It brings together in one book, as Lorene Pearson says, "the history, geography, sociology and anthropology" of northern New Mexico.[12] Still it is not a compendium of these disciplines, but a synthesis with all the fat rendered out; a lean book, it is the work of an artist rather than of a fact-gatherer. The work's conclusions depend as much on intuitive "feel" as on supporting research (though, as I have indicated, it contains plenty of that as well). Probably only a man like Fergusson, whose roots were deeply and sensitively embedded in Southwestern soil, could properly employ such a potentially dangerous method. But in *Rio Grande* the method is without doubt expertly used, with the result that the book is not only invaluable background material for a study of the writer's best fiction, but is also a splendidly readable and enlightening interpretive study of a region's long and colorful history.

II *A Novel of the Mountain Men*

Wolf Song, published in 1927, was the author's first fictional journey into Western history; and it remains one of his most effective and esthetically complete novels. And here, as is generally the case with Fergusson's historical fiction, the reader's appreciation for the work is richly enhanced by a reading of *Rio Grande.* The central character of *Wolf Song* is a mountain man; and, on the purely informational level, *Rio Grande* supplies a concise summary of the activities of mountain men in the southern Rockies during the 1830's and 1840's. The book also provides a thumbnail sketch of those character traits that the author associates with the typcial mountain man—traits that surely describe Sam Lash in *Wolf Song.* Such a man was basically an adventurer, someone with no ties to place or family. He roamed the wilderness—killing Indians, trapping beaver, and enjoying his grand isolation. Though he normally avoided the kinds of women who would want to marry him and bind him to an organized society, he occasionally indulged in short periods of intense dissipation. The mountain man plundered nature's bounty in order to support his extravagant way of life; and, in this sense, the author says in *Rio Grande,* he was "an instrument of expansion and conquest . . . the original go-getter" (147–49). His usefulness as a type, however, lasted only a few years since the supply of and demand for beaver soon diminished to virtually nothing.

In the 1830's, Taos was a popular base of operations for the mountain men. They sold their pelts there and squandered most of their money on women and liquor. "Taos whiskey and Taos women," Fergusson writes, "were known and talked about on every beaver stream in the Rockies. More than any other place Taos was the heart of the mountains."[13] At the beginning of *Wolf Song,* Sam Lash and two companions are returning to Taos after a year in the wilderness. A young giant with long blond hair, Sam is already a veteran trapper and mountain man. He had come from a large Kentucky family but, disliking the tame farmlands of the upper South, had headed West at an early age. Following a rough-and-tumble apprenticeship, he had earned a respected position among the mountain men, eagerly sharing their violent, reckless existence: "He could stand anything but comfort. He could do anything but rest. . . . When he hit a town, a trading post or a

rendezvous he was a creature of crying needs. . . . Riding into
a town he felt as though he could crunch its gathered human
sweetness between his teeth. And after a few days he would wake
up poor and sick, hating the smell of huddled sheltered men,
longing for mountains" (38). In the beginning at least, Sam Lash
appears a likely candidate to fulfill the trappers' credo, repeated
often in the novel: "a mountain man goes on until he gets rubbed
out" (40).

In Taos, Sam and a group of other mountain men sponsor a
baile (dance) to which they invite the town's citizenry. Predictably, after a keg of liquor has been consumed, a "ruction"
develops—a brawl in which the trappers are aligned against several dozen knife-wielding natives. For the mountain men, the
fight is a glorious outlet for pent-up tensions; and luckily they escape with only a few cuts and bruises. For Sam Lash, the evening is a turning point in his life: he dances with Lola Salazar, a
beautiful *rico* girl, and immediately falls in love with her. For
some time, prior to her meeting Sam, Lola, we are told, has
been discontented. She sits behind barred windows in the
Salazar house spinning fantasies of love and adventure. To marry
a man from another *rico* family, she realizes, would merely condemn her to re-enact her mother's fate: a monotonous existence
of sewing and gossiping while drinking chocolate and wine and
growing fat on rich foods. When she dances with Sam Lash, Lola
is overwhelmed by the trapper's strength and power; and her
prayers for a bold and exciting lover seem to have been answered.

Sam's courtship of the closely guarded Lola is a difficult and
brief affair, consisting mostly of a few stolen glances and words.
They manage to agree on a plan, however, by which Sam abducts
her and transports her to Bent's Fort (an outpost in southeastern
Colorado used by mountain men as a supply depot), where they
are married. Sam's friends are skeptical, but they consent to wait
for him to rejoin their trapping party at an agreed-upon rendezvous. After a ten-day honeymoon at Bent's Fort, Sam reluctantly
leaves his bride for another season of trapping beaver. At first, he
is happy to be once again alone in the wilderness. Slowly, however, his longing for Lola becomes almost unendurable. When he
reaches the rendezvous and finds that his colleagues
have gone without him, he makes a momentous decision: he will
return to Bent's Fort and to Lola.

On the return trip Sam's course is intersected by that of a Cheyenne warrior named Lone Wolf, who is searching for horses to give to a family of his tribe as his payment for marrying one of the family's daughters. Lone Wolf, a poor but valiant brave, had possessed nothing with which to purchase the maiden. He had consulted the tribe's medicine man, fasted for a week, and eventually been granted a vision of his destiny: make his fortune by stealing horses or die in the attempt. And now, ironically, he approaches a man who also is haunted by the image of a beloved woman; both Indian and Anglo, it seems, are singing "wolf songs which are always sung by lone warriors. Wolf songs are always about women for every lone warrior rides away from a woman" (161–62). Lone Wolf manages to steal Sam's horse and mule, but Sam tracks him; and, in the ensuing knife fight, the Indian is killed.

Ragged and wounded, Sam limps into Bent's Fort, only to discover that Lola's father has found her and taken her home. Returning to Taos, the trapper seeks the advice of a friendly priest who tells Sam that he would be more acceptable to the girl's family were he to become a Catholic and a citizen of Mexico. Sam, astonished but compliant, meekly agrees to these terms and is soon reunited with his wife: "He crushed her in his arms, and her face, backflung to meet his mouth, was a mask of willing pain. Antagonists who could neither triumph, they struggled in a grip neither could break . . ." (206). The priest also suggests that the elder Salazar, disgusted with the timidity of his own sons, will give Sam and Lola, as a dowry, a vast tract of wilderness across the mountains, a grant the Salazars have held for decades but have never settled. Sam is happy with this new challenge, for only a few days before he had seen the land and, not knowing whose it was, had thought that it "would have made a farm. . . . Here was timber and stone to build and land that would show black and rich under plow and water that would turn a mill and grass for a thousand cows . . ." (158).

Wolf Song is Fergusson's shortest novel; but, despite the book's brevity, its meanings are extraordinarily rich and suggestive. In the three major characters, Sam Lash, Lola Salazar, and Lone Wolf—representative of Anglo, Mexican-American, and Indian—the author explores the traditional triangle of Southwestern ethnic strife. In the encounters among the three cultures that are described in the novel, there is considerable friction and not a little violence. It should be noted immediately, however, that the resolution of conflict through marriage which Sam and Lola discover has scarcely been a common solution to racial problems in the Southwest—or elsewhere, for that matter. Indeed, Cecil Robinson raises the possibility that, "in creating the rebellious Lola," the author "was guilty of inserting an American mind into a Mexican woman."[14] To be sure, Lola is not the typical docile daughter that the *rico* families worked long and hard to produce. But she does accede to her father's demand that she return to Taos; and, in the end, the family wins a sizable victory in bending Sam to fit its inflexible customs. Sam and Lola's solution, in any event, is individual rather than ethnic or cultural; they are, in the final analysis, simply a man and woman who answer the ancient imperatives of blood and desire. The implications of their action, if there are any, they leave for others to analyze.

In a broader and more subtle sense Fergusson is also, in *Wolf Song* as in *Rio Grande,* employing Indian, Spaniard, and Anglo to illustrate his theories concerning primitive, Medieval, and modern cultures. Lone Wolf, who is said to belong to his tribe "as a bee belongs to its hive" (173), is a fitting representative of primitive man's unquestioning adherence to superstition and to the communal will. Lola may be rebellious, and therefore untypical; but the Salazar family, which is described at length, well illustrates the feudal, aristocratic values of a Medieval society. And Sam Lash, though partly assuming the savagery of the country he loves, never really sloughs off his cultural heritage; he possesses in abundance that practical capacity for organization and sustained action which is, Fergusson asserts, the special gift of modern man.

Sam, in fact, appears to be the only character in the novel who anticipates and responds adequately to changing conditions. The Indians cling to their primitive, nomadic way of life—a rigid reaction that inevitably conflicts with the advancing Anglo culture and results in the Indians' near annihilation. The *ricos* meanwhile lazily enjoy their rich, easy existence, and are blithely unaware that their moment of doom is almost within sight. (The realization that "the gringos were coming more every year with their wagonloads of cheap goods from St. Louis" [65] is the occasion for much scorn and ridicule among the *ricos,* but seems to them a fact hardly worth taking seriously.) Only Sam Lash recognizes that change is inevitable; he admits to himself that the days of the mountain men are numbered and that, if he is to survive, he must change his mode of living. At novel's end, therefore, he has resolved to take his wife into the wilderness to seek a new destiny for himself by developing the Salazar land grant.

Wolf Song, like all of the author's historical fiction, is grounded in an impressively thick layer of detail which lends the narrative an undeniable authenticity. The excellent descriptions of the characters' various ways of life issue, of course, from the same reading and research that, as I have indicated, are the basis of the nonfiction *Rio Grande*. In particular *Wolf Song* appears to rely heavily on *Life in the Far West*, George F. Ruxton's eyewitness account of the adventures of a group of celebrated mountain men.[15] A trapper named La Bonté, described by Ruxton, may well have been the model after which Sam Lash was created; in addition, the novel's central event, Sam's abduction of Lola, seems to have been suggested by a dramatic episode from *Life in the Far West* in which Dick Wooton, another mountain man described by Ruxton, kidnapped a Taos girl named Delores Salazar.[16] But, while Fergusson obviously borrowed facts, characters, and even incidents from his sources, the essence of the novel—the conflicting impulses in Sam to continue the wild, free life of the wilderness on the one hand and to establish a more orderly and human existence for himself on the other—is the author's own imaginative creation based on a conflict that Fergusson understood fully; for, as he indicates in *Home in the West*, he experienced at various times in his life similarly ambivalent emotions.

In regard to the dramatized conflict between wilderness and society, *Wolf Song* is a remarkable book, totally unlike most fiction set in the nineteenth-century West. In *Wolf Song*, as in *Footloose McGarnigal*, woman is used in her familiar symbolic role: as a sign of advancing civilization, a check and limit on male freedom. And here once again the author reverses the usual connotations of the female's role, sympathetically portraying her as a necessary balance to man's regressive tendencies—to the mountain man's childish desire, in this case, to shun all social responsibility. As opposed to the simplistic conclusions of the ordinary Western novel, *Wolf Song* projects a rich complexity, an interaction of conflicting impulses that, for Sam and Lola, results in a clear advance—though not necessarily a secure future. As man and wife, they remain "Antagonists who could neither triumph . . ." (206); but they are also partners in a joint venture

that might well succeed on a grand scale. The story ends hopefully, then, but not complacently; as in real life, a temporary victory does not ensure permanent happiness.

A final aspect of *Wolf Song* which deserves a brief comment is
its style. The language of the novel is lyrical and poetic, though
not lushly so. The author admits that, when he wrote the book,
he "was enamored of a swift and rhythmical style. I wanted intensity rather than bulk. I aspired to a sort of narrative poetry."[17]
In the first chapter, for example, we find a passage which describes the mountain men's entry into Taos (and which has been
included, incidentally, in several anthologies of Western literature); the passage well demonstrates the author's alliterative and
lyrical techniques: "Up from the edge of the prairie and over the
range rode three. Their buckskin was black with blood and shiny
from much wiping of greasy knives. . . . Hair hung thick to their
shoulders. Traps rattled in rucksacks . . ."(1).

Something about Southwestern history and landscape seemingly inspires poetry, and most of the region's writers at one time
or another indulge their taste for lyrical description. Fergusson,
for instance—though during his career he published only one
poem as such, a short lyric called "Timber Line" in the July,
1957, issue of *New Mexico Magazine*—once claimed that he had
written poetry all his life but had incorporated it into his prose,
his fiction especially, rather than into formal verse. In his fiction,
however, his is ordinarily a disciplined lyricism; and for certain
subjects—for the overtly romantic events of *Wolf Song,*
certainly—such a style seems appropriate. Undoubtedly A. B.
Guthrie's *The Big Sky,* a celebrated best seller several years ago
and a book still widely read, is the most famous novel yet written
about the Western trappers; but Guthrie's work, J. Frank Dobie
wrote, "does not talk to me or sing to me about the Mountain
Men as does Harvey Fergusson's *Wolf Song.*"[18] *Wolf Song,* as
Dobie's comment implies and as the book's title confirms, is as
much epic song as it is prose fiction; in that fact, I believe, lies
much of its power.

III   In Those Days

In Those Days, which appeared in 1929, is based in large
measure on the memoirs of the writer's maternal grandfather,
Franz Huning—reminiscences that Fergusson also used in *Home*

in the West to reconstruct his grandfather's biography. It is difficult to assess the extent to which the personality and emotional characteristics of Robert Jayson, the novel's central character, are modeled after those of Franz Huning, but the public careers of the two are obviously very similar. Like the author's grandfather, Jayson settles in Albuquerque after a long journey down the Santa Fe Trail, becomes a successful storekeeper and entrepreneur, and finally lapses into a bewildered old age. The subtitle of *In Those Days* is *An Impression of Change*; and Fergusson's purpose in writing the book, according to the introduction to *Followers of the Sun,* was to trace "the long curve of a human destiny"—to take an overview from which the forces which shaped that destiny might be more clearly discerned. The more chronologically detached our view, the author claims, the better we see that Jayson was merely a pawn in the cosmic chess game, that he was "dominated rather than dominating. Time and Change are the mighty characters in this story."[19] Appropriately, Jayson's personal history parallels the development from freight wagons to railroads to automobiles of the Southwest itself; thus the novel attempts to comment on regional as well as on individual change.

Like many young men in the nineteenth century, Robert Jayson abandons his home in the East—Connecticut, in his case—shortly after the Civil War and goes West, because "West was the way out of everything. West was the home of hope."[20] He reluctantly leaves Elizabeth, his sweetheart, behind and sets out to make his fortune, promising to send for her later. Following a rugged trip over the Santa Fe Trail, he finds himself in the Spanish village of Albuquerque, where he decides, more or less by default, to stay. He gets a job as clerk in a store owned by Abel Doxey, a shrewd and demanding master; and Jayson's experiences in Doxey's store prove to be a valuable apprenticeship. In most small Southwestern towns in the nineteenth century the general store was a powerful institution. The Spanish-speaking natives, most of whom were unaccustomed to dealing with money or basic arithmetic, were from their earliest years deeply in debt to the storekeeper; and the owner's delicate exercise of the financial and political leverage afforded by his position became something of a local art form. Jayson, under the tutelage of Abel Doxey, learns his lesson well.

When Jayson arrives in Albuquerque, he is a painfully naive

and inexperienced young man. He believes that "life was a thing of toil and blood and he had never before tasted either" (11). A "shy, misplaced-looking stranger" (23), he idles away his evenings sitting in the corner of the saloon, neither drinking nor speaking to any of the customers. As time passes, however, he begins to make friends. He strikes up an acquaintanceship with Tom Foote, a seasoned veteran of the Southwest and also an employee of Abel Doxey's. He is befriended by Diego Aragon, scion of the town's most venerable *rico* family (and a character whose eventual decline and decay seem almost a mirror image of the fate of Diego Delcasar, Ramon's uncle in *The Blood of the Conquerors*). After much hesitation and soul-searching, Jayson allows his landlady's daughter to initiate him into the delights of sex; and he soon acquires a taste for the many brown, willing girls who seem to await his pleasure.

Despite his doubts, Jayson decides, when he tires of working for Doxey, to go along with a scheme hatched by his friend Tom Foote—an expedition into Apache country to trade cheap trinkets for horses and mules that the Indians have stolen in Mexico. "When everything comes easy," Tom tells him, "you jest rot" (44); and Jayson, reluctantly agreeing to the truth of that statement, resolves to risk his comfortable life and small savings in the hope of quick gain. In Jayson, the author says, a longing to cling to "easy ways fought unsuccessfully against an impulse to move, risk, suffer, win big or lose all" (63). The trading itself proceeds smoothly, but the expedition, which had not set out until late summer, encounters on the return trip a blinding snowstorm.

Half-starved, the men straggle into Albuquerque a few days before Christmas; but, though half their stock was lost in the storm, profits from the venture allow Jayson and Foote to open a small store on the town square in competition with Abel Doxey's establishment. In time, the store prospers; and the partners begin supplying their own goods by sponsoring freight caravans on the Santa Fe Trail. On one of these trips Jayson arranges for Elizabeth to meet him in St. Louis, where they are married. Both have changed, however, and in particular Elizabeth's fear and hatred of the country that her husband now loves erects a wall of constraint between them. On the journey to New Mexico, Elizabeth is killed during an attack by renegade Indians, an occurrence for which Jayson feels guilt and remorse the remainder of his life.

Years pass, and Jayson becomes a wealthy man, branching out
into a variety of enterprises. He acquires a sawmill in the mountains and a silver mine in Socorro, a village south of Albuquerque. "He gutted mountains and stripped them. He raped the
earth. He lived in a rush of power visibly conquering rock and
tree, making wheels turn and men sweat. And his power grew on
its own conquest. More money, more things to do . . ." (143).
Nearing forty, he reaches the height of his financial prowess. At
this crucial juncture, the railroads come to Albuquerque, plung-
ing the town—Jayson included—into a frenzy of euphoric ambition. For a time, the aging Jayson intends to form a profitable al-
liance by marrying into a prominent local railroad family, but
marries instead Annie Latz, his housekeeper's daughter and a girl
half his age.

He and Annie are happy, but over the years his hopes of becoming a tycoon are slowly dissipated. His silver and timber play
out, and the opening of newer and more specialized shops forces
the closing of his old-fashioned general store. When first Tom
Foote and then Annie die around the turn of the century, the last
of Jayson's ambitions die with them. With the initial appearance
in town of automobiles, Jayson sees in the strange contraptions a
symbol of the brave new world that he can neither understand
nor condemn. Though "he never lost the thrill of wielding
money, of seeing money grow" (196), he now seems content to
relax and daydream about the glorious excitement of his youth.
He gracefully adopts a new role—that of "old-timer," one of the
town's first Anglo settlers and a participant in unimaginable adventures. Some of the community's younger men seek him out to
hear his reminiscences, and he willingly obliges them with tales
drawn from a now remote past. He has few regrets about the
course of his life, but he sometimes feels that he is a displaced
person, a relic from the past that has hardened but not quite
died. He gradually settles, at any rate, into "that mood of calm
unreasonable acceptance of everything"—an attitude which makes
"catastrophes and triumphs look for the moment just alike" and
"the future a matter of the utmost unconcern" (266).

Robert Jayson, like his actual predecessor Franz Huning, is not
so much a businessman as a merchant-adventurer, a trader,
whose success is rooted in the peculiar conditions of the old
Southwest. He believes that the railroad offers him an opportunity to become a millionaire, but in reality it is, for him, an in-

strument of doom: it brings to town businessmen and business practices that he is unable to adapt to. For Jayson, then, both success and failure are largely the results of circumstances he cannot control. But, on an individual basis, the author believes, either a man must consciously strive for success or he must consent to failure; and certainly Jayson's personal responses to changing conditions complement the workings of these implacable circumstances.

Even as a young man Jayson's adjustment to change—that is, in Fergusson's terms, the achieving of an internal equilibrium that allows the individual to seize opportunities—is a long and arduous struggle. He is by nature a sentimentalist, and his sympathies for stray animals and stray humans are easily aroused. The responsibility he feels for his first wife's death instills in him an enduring remorse—always, according to Fergusson, a spurious emotion. And, long before his old age, he indulges in nostalgic longings to return to the past. But Jayson is aware of these dangerous tendencies within himself, and for several decades he manages to combat them. When old age finally deprives him of the will to struggle, he slips into that stasis which is in effect the end of life—for Jayson, the condition toward which all his natural inclinations had always pointed him.

Jayson has been, however, active and in many ways successful; and there is no hint of censure in Fergusson's description of his declining years. Because he has worked hard and achieved much, the author rewards him with a measure of gentle tolerance (rather than the scorn Fergusson ordinarily heaps on irredeemable failures). It is one thing for an old man like Robert Jayson to retire from the world and allow younger men to advance to positions of wealth and power; it is quite another for someone as vigorous and talented as Ramon Delcasar in *The Blood of the Conquerors* to retreat into a vegetable existence of changeless ease.

Here again, Jayson closely resembles the merchant-adventurer Franz Huning, as Fergusson describes him in *Home in the West*. Huning as a youth imaginatively pursued adventure and change, became a wealthy storekeeper and businessman in his middle age, and in his later years retired to the library of his castle-like home in Albuquerque, where he read and studied and shut himself off from a society he no longer understood or admired. But Huning earned his seclusion, Fergusson admits, with the accomplishments of an active life; and the same might well be said of Jayson. For most men, the cycle of destiny is a pattern of suspense, stuggle, triumph—and disappointment. And, since an individual's hopes can never be fulfilled completely, disappointment is just as much a part of the cycle as is occasional triumph—a fact that Jayson, like Huning, finally acknowledges.

In Those Days is the weakest of Fergusson's historical novels. A central problem, as one critic has suggested, is "the story's episodic structure, which unhappily transforms each of the episodes of Jayson's life from a realized fictional moment into a concealed statement that time passes on."[21] Because the novel is not really lengthy enough to show "the long curve of a human destiny," the author's avowed purpose, Fergusson compromises by pinpointing four crucial phases of his main character's career. The result of this compromise is a rather choppy, disjointed narrative which summarizes but does not adequately illustrate the passage of time. As is the case with *The Life of Riley*, the writer simply tries to cover too long a span—the *life* of Riley, the *life* of Robert Jayson—in too brief a space.

Still, *In Those Days* is a readable and sometimes illuminating tale. Fergusson suppresses in it his tendency to comment explicitly and at length on his character's behavior; the writer objectively describes Jayson's thoughts and actions and invites the reader to draw his own conclusions concerning them. To be sure, those thoughts and actions conform to the theoretical framework outlined above; but the reader, rather than being constantly reminded of the author's backstage presence, is allowed to focus his attention squarely on character and incident rather than on the philosophical points they raise. This circumstance in itself, it seems to me, is a clear, self-evident advance over the narrative method of Fergusson's previous novels. In addition, *In Those Days*, as is true of most of the writer's historical fiction, contains much interesting and authentic information which is deftly worked into the usual business of the novel. Fergusson is a superb reporter of historical details, and his descriptions of Spanish *ricos* and Anglo freighters, frontier storekeepers and railroad men come alive with a vividness that few modern American chroniclers of the nineteenth-century West can match.

An Impression of Change, as I have indicated, is the fitting subtitle of *In Those Days;* but it is also, I think, an appropriate epigraph to all the author's historical novels. Fergusson believed that the record of man's life on earth—all history, that is, not just Southwestern history—is a story of change and of the individual's either meeting or failing to meet its challenge. When a man resists the current of change, he and the institutions of which he is a part become rigid and inflexible; and they are no longer viable. In *Rio Grande*, the writer shows how cultures wither and die when they attempt to outlive their usefulness. In *Wolf Song* and *In Those Days*, he demonstrates the premise in terms of individual lives.

Sam Lash perceives that the mountain men are rapidly becoming anachronisms; and he will be duly rewarded, it is implied, for his far-sighted decision to abandon the only mode of life he knows and build a new existence for himself on the Salazar land grant. Robert Jayson prospers as long as he adapts himself to meet altered conditions; he thickens into immobility when age robs him of his ability to change. But Jayson enjoys a long and fruitful life, and the author seems tacitly to admit that he well deserves his placid old age—his recessional of imperturbable serenity. Fergusson is perhaps saying, then, through the character of Jayson, that in the lives of men—as in the lives of cultures—there arrives a point when it is no longer possible or desirable to compete with the strength and vigor of youth, and that the individual must recognize that point and learn to grow old gracefully.

CHAPTER 7

The Conqueror

THE arc of Fergusson's course as a novelist was somewhat unusual in that it reached its apogee at its conclusion. There are, of course, exceptions to any generalization concerning the writer's canon; but, on the whole, his fiction, examined chronologically, displays a steady progress in quality with the result that the last of his published works—*Grant of Kingdom* and *The Conquest of Don Pedro*—are unquestionably the finest achievements of a lengthy and distinguished career. Too often, it seems, promising young American writers attain an early success, only to enter a long decline in which their subsequent books are merely reworkings of the plot and character formulas that first brought them fame. Fergusson avoided this pitfall. Since none of his works was a genuine best seller, he was spared, to a great extent, the temptation of pandering to popular tastes.[1] Still, the author's greatest financial success, as well as the highest incidence of encouragement and critical praise of his books, occurred early in his career—during the 1920's, to be specific—and it is testimony, I believe, to the depth of his talent and self-discipline that he continued to grow and mature as artist and craftsman long after the first wave of enthusiasm for his works had ebbed.

Grant of Kingdom and *The Conquest of Don Pedro*, like *Wolf Song* and *In Those Days,* are set in the nineteenth-century Southwest and are fictional studies of the effects of change on individual men and their society. In a sense, these novels hark back to their predecessors in that *Grant of Kingdom* seems to continue the story of Sam Lash where *Wolf Song* drops it, while *The Conquest of Don Pedro* treats the same general subject matter as *In*

Those Days. But, rather than being simply hollow echoes of earlier books, the later novels are fuller and richer versions of basic storylines that suggest infinite variations and extensions.

In *Grant of Kingdom* and in *The Conquest of Don Pedro* all the scattered attributes of the author's fiction—sense of place, purposeful conception and execution, a style as clear and sparkling as a mountain trout stream—seem to converge in heightened form; and the results are books which, in technique and esthetic effect, approach perfection. The author's literary labors paid many dividends during his long career—but none greater than his final two novels. In these works Fergusson confirms his claim as artistic "conqueror," just as the stories' major characters are revealed as conquerors of their social environment.

I   *The Struggle for a Kingdom*

Grant of Kingdom, which appeared in 1950, broke a thirteen-year fictional drought for the writer; he had not published a novel since *The Life of Riley* in 1937. *Grant of Kingdom* is, on several levels, a remarkable book. One interesting feature, which catches the eye immediately, is the circumstance that the book offers its own philosophical interpretation—a brief Author's Note which precedes the text. A primary tenet of Fergusson's theory of fiction is that absolute clarity is a goal to be prized and striven for (a point at which he parted company with a great many other modern writers). He believed that an explicit statement of purpose by a novelist is a useful service to readers who might otherwise remain perplexed and uncertain. He first experimented with this device in the introduction to *Followers of the Sun*, which provides invaluable comments on three of his fictions; and the prefatory note to *Grant of Kingdom* contains similarly helpful guidelines to a proper reading of the narrative which follows. In that foreword, the writer says that in the 1920's he visited a lovely valley in northern New Mexico, where he saw the ruins of a magnificent house once owned by a man who had ruled the surrounding countryside. Though he does not specify the location, Fergusson obviously refers to the fabled Maxwell Land Grant, a tract of nearly two million acres centering on the town of Cimarron, which was ceded to Carlos Beaubien and held during the middle decades of the nineteenth century by his son-in-law, Lucien Maxwell.

Through library research and interviews with old-timers, the author reconstructed a tale that entered his imagination and eventually issued into the novel *Grant of Kingdom*. Though the fiction does not adhere closely to fact, Fergusson claims that he derived both plot and theme from actual events. There were four key participants in those events, he says, "each of whom had achieved his moment of power in that dominion and by reason of that royal grant. . . ."[2] He continues:

Here, it seemed to me, was a struggle for power in a small but complete society, isolated by distance and wilderness, which had much in common with the greater power struggles that periodically shake the world. Here were the benevolent autocrat creating order, the power-hungry egoist destroying it, the warrior tragically bound to his weapon, the idealist always in conflict with an irrational world, struggling to save his own integrity. The chief purpose of the book is to portray these four men, each in his turn and in his moment of crisis—to trace him back to his origins and see him in the making, to show the form and meaning of his destiny. (vi)

The first man who attempts to subdue the awesome tract of wilderness is Jean Ballard, a character very similar to Sam Lash in *Wolf Song*. Ballard, a son of a Scotch-Irish father and French-Catholic mother, leaves his Kentucky home as a young man to join the ranks of the Western trappers. He enjoys the wild, free life of the mountain men but, unlike most of his colleagues, feels with growing urgency an impulse to settle and build. When he first sees the beautiful Consuelo Coronel of Taos, he is thirty-three years old; and his destiny becomes immediately obvious to him. Ballard is a man "who felt deeply the need of woman, not merely as a complement to his flesh, but as an anchor to the earth and a center of his being. For man alone may be a conqueror but everything that lasts is built around a woman" (30). In the face of that "massive, inert resistance" (32) erected by the girl's conservative *rico* family against anything new or strange, he is at first helpless; but with Consuelo's active connivance, she becomes pregnant by Ballard; and they are allowed to marry.

As a dowry, Don Tranquilino, Consuelo's father, gives them a parchment, inscribed by the king of Spain, which details the boundaries of an enormous block of land across the mountains, granted to the Coronel family for service to the crown. With his wife, child, and a half-dozen laborers, Ballard leaves the safety of

Taos to settle his wilderness grant. He first concludes a treaty
with the Ute Indians, who will allow him to live in peace provided he helps protect them from the warlike tribes of the Great
Plains. Then, in a beautiful valley in the foothills of the Sangre de
Cristo Mountains, he builds a great house. For a time, failure
seems a distinct possibility since Ballard and his wife, in order to
establish their empire, must battle the elements, predatory animals, and marauding Indians. Eventually, though, their vast
herds of sheep and cattle make them rich; and Ballard becomes
"the absolute ruler of a minor kingdom, strictly feudal in its social
structure" (97). The "benevolent autocrat," he rigorously maintains order throughout his domain. Indian hunters, Mexican
sheepherders, and Texan ranchmen are all welcome on the land
as long as they conform to the master's rules of conduct. The
hospitality of the great house, dominated by Consuelo, becomes
legendary; no one is ever turned away from it hungry, and there
are often as many as a hundred guests sitting down to an evening
meal at Ballard's table.

Ballard's heyday, which lasts about two decades, begins in the
1850's and ends in the late 1870's. By the 1870's, railroads and
money have begun to invade the Southwest; and these agents of
modern technology and capitalism work an irrevocable change in
the region: they "destroyed one kind of man and created another"
(144). They bring to northern New Mexico such men as the
money- and power-hungry Major Arnold Newton Blore, who
wrests control of the grant from an aged and diseased Ballard.
Blore—the "egoist"—is "a dedicated man, as saints and poets are
dedicated men. He wanted power and he sacrificed everything
else to that end . . ." (178). A Confederate veteran, Blore possesses a lust for power that springs from his childhood status as a
poor white in the class-conscious South; and he discovers in the
newly opened West a formative society in which he may freely
indulge his savage ambitions. For him, one of the secret attrac-
tions of the Ballard grant is that it affords him an opportunity to
become a snobbish and despotic landowner—one cut from the
mold of those plantation aristocrats whom as a child he had both
envied and despised. When Blore finds that Ballard, in an attempt to maintain his lavish scale of living, has sunk hopelessly
into debt, he persuades the latter's creditors to file suit. Then, on
behalf of a syndicate of Denver financiers, he offers Ballard a fair

price for his holdings, an offer the great man, now mortally ill, must accept.

Because the language of the original royal document is exceedingly vague, Blore is able to bribe government surveyors to increase the official dimensions of his property, after which he partitions the grant into small ranches and implants the beginnings of a town. He also brings in Clay Tighe, a celebrated Dodge City lawman, to impose order on his empire. Tighe is "the warrior" whose sole proficiency is the dexterity with which he handles his weapons. He sincerely wishes to be fair and to promote peace and justice, but ultimately his only tool is a gun; his only method of achieving his ends, violence. When "squatters" and small landholders in the area threaten to combat the shenanigans of the grant's new owners with vigilante action, Tighe tries to avert trouble with talk and compromise; in the end, however, he is forced to gun down two of the malcontents—a dramatic demonstration of skill that not only defeats the rebels' plans but securely establishes the marshall's reputation among the townspeople.

Roughly the last quarter of the novel is concerned with the "idealist," as Fergusson calls him in the "Author's Note"—a strange backwoods preacher named Daniel Laird. Laird, born in the hills of Tennessee, leaves his native region and roams westward, finally settling on the Ballard grant where he works for many years as a carpenter. His greatest asset is a deep, commanding voice which he uses to lead a weekly devotional service of singing and Bible reading. Generally, though, he avoids other humans—especially women. When Blore assumes control, Laird opposes as best he can the ruthless tactics of the new owners and is branded a troublemaker for his efforts. But a more serious threat to Laird's peace of mind is his growing passion for Betty Weiss, whom Blore has imported to run the local hotel and bawdy house; and Betty in turn is attracted to the handsome preacher. In a desperate "flight, not only from this place but from human society" (269), Laird escapes into the mountains. During a snowstorm, he is tempted to surrender to a peaceful death; but he slowly recovers his will to live—"to regain a contact with his fellow beings" (276).

Revitalized, Laird returns to civilized life, marries Betty, and moves to Colorado where he becomes a successful rancher and

politician. As a radical member of the state legislature, he thun-
ders "in his mighty voice against the trusts and Wall Street, pre-
dicting the day when humble men who worked with their hands
would rise in their organized power and smite the mighty"
(301–02). Laird is unquestionably the book's dominant character,
and he lodges himself in the reader's mind more stubbornly than
Blore, Tighe, or even Ballard; certainly he is morally superior to
the first two and more humanly believable than the legendary
ruler of the grant. Though Laird's relationship to the land grant is
somewhat peripheral—and his claim to the writer's attention,
therefore, is perhaps not so secure as that of several other people
in the book—he becomes one of Fergusson's most completely
realized characters, a symbol of spiritual and physical renewal and
an affirmation of life's ultimate meaning.

Laird, however, though he may be the exemplary hero, is not
the author's spokesman in the novel; that role is reserved for
James Lane Morgan, a young lawyer who comes to the West in
the 1870's with tuberculosis and who witnesses, with fascination
and a measure of sadness, the spectacle of change then occurring
on the Ballard grant. Morgan is intelligent and reflective, and his
"recollections" are an important segment of the narrative; they
should be considered, I think, the author's commentary on his
own tale. The pattern of Morgan's life is very similar to that of
Fergusson's experiences, as the author describes them in *Home
in the West*. Morgan loves the Southwest's beauty and lack of social and legal restraint, but he eventually decides that his true
destiny lies in the great cities of the East. "I was evading my
proper destiny," he tells us. "I knew what kept me in the West
was a love of physical freedom, adventure and excitement. . . .
My adult business was back in New York, and I finally returned,
to assume the management of my father's business, to practice
law and finally to become a judge . . ." (300). Concerning the
other characters, Morgan adopts a philosophical attitude. They
too, he decides, were only following the dictates of their destinies: "I have been impressed all my life," he writes, "by the
fact that no man can escape the inner drive of his destiny. Whatever kind of power is in him, that must he use, for better or
worse, and even though it consume or destroy him" (303).

Shortly after the turn of the twentieth century, Morgan revisits
the locale where as a young man he acquired health and experi-

ence. He learns of the fate of people he had known: Laird's success, Ballard's death following the sale of the grant, Tighe's assassination by rustlers. He finds that Blore after a couple of years had resold the land at an enormous profit and returned to Denver, where he continued to accumulate vast sums of money until his death. On the grant itself he discovers Ballard's great house in ruins; Blore's town, moreover, is almost deserted, its doom having been assured when the railroad passed it by. Morgan's nostalgic epilogue is a fitting recessional, a reminder that regions, like men, have their life cycles: some of the human characters adjusted to change and prospered, but after a half-century of being the scene of furious conflict and exploitation the land seemed to have taken on the aspect of a tired old man; it had aged and wished only to be left alone. In the town, Morgan seeks out the few who still remember the glories of a vanished world, and they exchange memories of shared experiences:

To me the droning tales of these old-timers had the quality of elegy. I felt as though I were witnessing the process by which the past becomes a beloved myth, simplified in memory that one may see the meanings that are always obscured by the noise and dust of the present. The sleepy inertia of the little town made its past seem truly heroic. In the days when I had known it and before, a great gust of passion and energy had struck this place and blown itself out and left in its wake the ruin of a proud house and a legend in the memories of aging men. (310–11)

Inevitably a passage such as the one just quoted has given rise to attempts to make Fergusson's historical novels conform to the theories of the so-called "myth critics."[3] But the author, in *Grant of Kingdom* as elsewhere in his fiction, is concerned not so much with exploring the literary possibilities of legend and myth as with illustrating those philosophical precepts expounded in *Modern Man* and *People and Power*. For example, *Grant of Kingdom*, as Fergusson clearly states in the foreword, is a study in microcosm of the dynamics of social, political, and financial power. For his day and his world, Ballard is a great leader, such as the prototypical leader described in *People and Power*: he is a man of superior emotional balance and extraordinary abilities who in the natural course of things rises above the mass of common humanity. Ballard's hunger for power is disciplined by belief in a great ideal—the principle of order and community. He brings peace, prosperity, and civilization to his grant; and his life's labor results in advancement for an entire region. But Ballard, by the time he dies, is no longer a leader: he is simply a relic of the past.

When he becomes a member of the Coronel family and accepts their grant, Ballard is obliged to adopt a medieval life style. He is transformed into a feudal baron, *el patron;* and he establishes order by means of personal loyalty, rather than by smoothly functioning organization. He has no business sense and distrusts banks and risky investments; it is inevitable, therefore, that he runs afoul of the go-for-broke economics that settle over the West in the latter decades of the nineteenth century. For Ballard late in life, "Work and physical danger are simple things to deal with. What makes life hard is the bewilderment of change and complication, the rush of people and money, the impact of unexpected things . . ." (153).

At this point Major Blore, the "modern man," enters the story. He understands the importance of proper organization, and he knows how to use money and technology. Blore delights in toppling so exalted an aristocrat as Jean Ballard; and, as Cecil Robinson rightly points out, he is blood kin in this regard to Faulkner's rapacious Snopes clan, who gleefully and inexorably undermine the old ruling class of Yoknapatawpha County.[4] But, while Blore is ruthless and almost psychopathic in his lust for power, he is also, as James Lane Morgan affirms, "a man of great ability" (301). Perhaps the net result of Blore's influence on the land is a slight gain; certainly he attempts (from selfish motives, to be sure) to usher the grant and its human inhabitants into the modern world and thus to save both from ruin and decay.

If Ballard is the medieval man and Blore the modern man, the character who bridges the gap is Daniel Laird. At first, Laird, who sympathizes wholly with Ballard, wishes only to find his just ranking in the feudal order and to serve his master as a proper retainer. He is an idealist, who approaches life with many preconceptions (rather than flexibly and patiently—the proper attitudes, according to Fergusson, of a truly well-balanced man). Predictably, Laird's mistaken assumptions concerning mankind's behavior and capacities are finally demolished, smashed to bits by recalcitrant human nature. When the grant is sold, he flees to the mountains where he gradually comes to understand that, by retreating into the beauty and tranquility of nature, "he had tried to go back to his own childhood—to the remembered peace of long ago" (275). He also realizes now that the individual must compromise and accept life as it is offered to him; he must change to meet changing conditions. Laird, we perceive, is an individual of great inner strength who has never achieved fulfillment because he has never surrendered to—never fully understood—his destiny. After his struggles in the valley and in the mountains, his proper role is revealed to him; and his response to this revelation is to enter the arena of modern power politics; as a result, he is amply rewarded in both financial and human terms. Laird, then, is not only one of the writer's most expertly drawn characters but also an effective embodiment of his creator's philosophical ideals.

Grant of Kingdom, though a moving and highly convincing novel, is not without a few technical flaws. For one thing, Fergusson's now familiar problems with plot development arise once again to cause difficulty. The narrative simply encompasses too lengthy a time span and too many characters to be a fully integrated work of art. The author employs here, however, an unusual structural device which mitigates somewhat the impact of this weakness: rather than stringing the narrative thread along the sometimes aimless path of a single human life, he uses the grant itself as the work's principal unifying agent. The grandeur of the land and the magnificent sweep of its panoramic history allow us largely to overlook technical defects. Still, there is considerable justice in Lorene Pearson's complaint that too much of the book is "in essay form."[5] Or, more accurately, it is in the form of historical exposition; because he tries to cover so much of the natural and human landscape, the author is often forced to summarize rather than to portray dramatically.

But, when all its flaws have been tallied and duly assessed, *Grant of Kingdom* remains a powerful work—a rival to *The Conquest of Don Pedro* for the honor of being judged the writer's best novel. Technically, I believe, two facets of the book account for its esthetic effectiveness: tone and tempo. As I have indicated, *Grant of Kingdom* may be read as an *exemplum* of the writer's theories of human behavior and social organization, but the tone of the book is mellow and warm; there is in it none of the harsh stridency of the authorial proclamations that punctuate his earlier

fiction. In *Home in the West*, Fergusson admits that the anti-
social wanderings of his youth engendered in him very early in
life a skeptical disdain for his fellow humans. "Only sympathy,"
he writes, "makes the human spectacle tolerable and finally fascinating, even at its worst, but in me sympathy was a slow
growth and a late one" (95). Nowhere, however, are the fruits of
that late growth more attractively and convincingly displayed than
in this novel, and in *The Conquest of Don Pedro* which follows it.
In *Grant of Kingdom*, moreover, the writer, through the arrangement of events and even more through a lean and supple
prose, evokes precisely the right tempo. J. Frank Dobie, I think,
has phrased it best: the novel, Dobie says, though perhaps defective in some respects, succeeds because it brings together the
unique tempos of both "earth and metal."[6] It moves not only to the
leisurely pace of a great pastoral kingdom, but also to the clan-
gorous urgency of invading money and machinery. With grace
and wisdom, the novel suggests both the tragic disruption and
the hopeful promise of time and change. Not many recent American novels, I venture, have achieved as much.

II   *The Capture of a Town*

If *Grant of Kingdom* describes a series of impressively brave
and heroic figures in Southwestern history, *The Conquest of Don
Pedro* depicts a different kind of hero—a "conqueror" who
triumphs by thought and patience, but one whose accomplishments are just as important to the region's development as those
of the men of action. The novel's central character is Leo
Mendes, who, like Robert Jayson in *In Those Days*, is a member
of that fraternity of Southwestern merchant-adventurers to which
the author's grandfather belonged. Leo is an invader of sorts; he
contributes "nothing to the conquest of the wilderness, but for
the business of penetrating a human society he had certain gifts
which were not common among American pioneers."[7] A gentle,
reflective Jewish peddler, he abhors violence and declines to
carry a gun, even in a society where weapons are ubiquitous.
    Leo admits that he is something of a fatalist; his rationale for
not keeping a gun is that "If there's a bullet with my name on it
I'll stop it anyway . . . I believe that what's going to happen is
going to happen" (162). He calmly accepts the circumstance that

"a man's destiny is a thing he discovers, a mystery that unfolds, and he pursued his ends always in a spirit of inquiry rather than of heroic determination" (7). One of the things that makes Leo such a formidable antagonist in business and in love is his fatalistic resignation to what has to be, combined with an unflinching competitiveness. His "conquest" is the establishment of a store in the village of Don Pedro, a small native town a few miles north of El Paso. The title of the book is not merely ironic—though there is probably a touch of irony in it—for in a sense Leo's achievement is indeed a conquest. He is not ostentatiously heroic in the manner of Sam Lash or Jean Ballard; his virtues are patience and a quiet determination, by means of which he penetrates, more completely than he ever could have by physical bluster, the town's rigid feudal society.

As a Portuguese Jew—and to some extent a reincarnation of the legendary "wandering Jew"—Leo proves to be an appropriate and provocative figure through which the author explores the social structure and mores of the nineteenth-century Southwest. Having dark skin and hair, Leo is sometimes mistaken for a Mexican; yet his ethnic and cultural experience creates in him a conviction that to the end he will remain essentially an outsider, an interloper in a Christian society: "At heart he was always and everywhere a stranger, with the reticence, the detachment and skepticism of the man who can mingle in any society but feels he belongs to none" (4). From this position he observes, sympathetically but objectively, the human carnival that surrounds him, patiently awaiting at the same time a revelation of his own destiny.

A native of New York City, Leo as a young man contracts tuberculosis and shortly after the Civil War abandons his job as a bookkeeper and migrates to New Mexico. He becomes a peddler, trading among the villagers of the upper Rio Grande valley near Santa Fe. At first, he fears and despises the wild country over which he travels. But, as he becomes more sure of himself and as his health is restored, he learns to love the Southwestern mountains and deserts; indeed, he gradually achieves a communion with nature that partakes of the pantheism of Spinoza, whose philosophy he admires. For several years Leo is content with his life as a wandering peddler. In a village of *ladrones* (thieves), he enters into a profitable arrangement whereby he sells on commission the villagers' merchandise, most of it stolen in Mexico; and by this means he accumulates a sizable bank account. One evening sitting in the plaza of Santa Fe, a town he employs as his base of operations, Leo is transfixed by the gaze of a handsome young woman whose name, he later learns, is Delores Pino; Delores, who lives a solitary existence, is rumored to be a witch and fortune-teller. Leo follows Delores to her small dwelling, where she assures him that she does not possess supernatural powers. Nevertheless, she foretells his future, prophesying great changes in his life. "Perhaps," she concludes, "you are a man of many lives" (77). In this manner there begins a mutually satisfying affair between two lonely and isolated people.

As time passes, Leo increasingly feels a necessity to alter his mode of living, but he cannot arrive for a while at a firm decision. Then, on one of his trips to Santa Fe, he discovers that Delores has mysteriously disappeared, perhaps has been run out of town or even murdered by one of her many enemies. Leo believes that this is an omen, a confirmation of his destiny: he will leave the familiar terrain of northern New Mexico and move to the southern part of the territory, in the lower river valley, where he will invest his savings in a general store in the town of Don Pedro.

Once there, he faces many obstacles in Don Pedro, the most difficult being the Vierras, the town's ruling *rico* family. The Vierras maintain a storeroom at the rear of their house from which they supply, at inflated prices, the basic necessities for the area's native population, most of whom are deeply in debt to the *ricos*. Leo, however, shrewdly brings into his business as partner Aurelio Baltran, the Vierras' most unrelenting enemy. With the fierce Aurelio guarding his person, Leo has little to fear from possible violent reprisal.

Slowly Leo's *Tienda Barata* (cheap store) prospers. He befriends the town's powerful Italian priest, Padre Orlando, who is, like himself, a transplanted New Yorker. With the tacit approval of the Church's representative in the town, he easily attracts most of the area's common people to his establishment; and he earns their good will by lending money to those of their number who wish to become independent ranchers and sheepherders. Because of his obvious skills as accountant and businessman, he assumes the role of banker and financial adviser to many of the great families of the lower valley, thereby becoming one of the few

Anglos in the area to be invited to their social gatherings. Leo's store eventually becomes a celebrated trading center for much of the Southwest and northern Mexico.

But Leo's final triumph is signaled only when Don Augustin Vierra, a reckless man with no sense of the value of money, loses most of his operating capital in a poker game and is forced to obtain a loan from Leo; his "conquest" is confirmed when Lupe, Don Augustin's wife, involves him in a sexual intrigue. Leo is now a success, and "success anywhere and any time," the author tells us, "is always the same thing—a sudden focusing of human energies and passions and demands upon its victim" (82). Leo, a power in his own little world, finds himself enmeshed in a web of hard work and growing responsibility. In a symbolic action of great significance, he exchanges his burro, a valued companion during his days as a peddler, for a three-hundred-dollar Kentucky saddle horse. To the poor people, he becomes "Don Leo"—a recognized *rico*, even though he never feels that he actually belongs to that class.

When Leo first opened his store in Don Pedro, the establishment was haunted from the beginning by the Vierras' adopted daughter, Magdalena. A rebellious child who dislikes the restrictive atmosphere of the Vierra house, Magdalena enjoys the freedom and opportunity afforded by the store. Leo for his part is careful not to offend her, and the two are soon friends and allies. In a few years Magdalena, still a child, is sent away to a convent school in Santa Fe; when she returns, she is sixteen—a ripe and beautiful young woman. Leo, though he is nearing forty, is smitten by her beauty; and Magdalena, contemptuous of her Mexican suitors, suggests that she and Leo be married in a civil ceremony (since Leo refuses to convert to Catholicism, there can be no Church wedding). Leo assents, and for more than two years they are a happy and fulfilled couple. Their house becomes an institution in the lower valley; it is a gathering place for Mexican aristocrats and Anglo ranchers and soldiers—a meeting ground where the two cultures can come together in peace and friendship.

The ordered tranquility of Don Leo's world, however, is destroyed by the intrusion of Texan broncobuster and horse-trainer Bob Coppinger. Though they have little in common, Leo and Coppinger become friends. Coppinger is immediately dazzled by Magdalena, and he is soon hopelessly in love with her; even worse, it becomes increasingly apparent to Leo that Magdalena loves the tall Texan. This situation reaches a climax because of a salt lake a few miles from Don Pedro, just across the Texas border. For decades the lake, considered by custom and Mexican law to be public property, has supplied salt to the area's poor people. Now, however, it is owned by the state of Texas and may be seized by anyone able to defend it. Coppinger, desperate to impress Magdalena, resolves to claim the lake and exact tribute from those who use it. Because of this threatened action, tempers flare; and bloodshed seems imminent for a time. As in Fergusson's imaginative treatment of the story of the Maxwell Land Grant in *Grant of Kingdom,* the writer here again makes good use of a famous incident in Southwestern history: the El Paso Salt War, in which several people were killed in a dispute over possession of a salt lake to the east of El Paso.

Leo is anguished by Magdalena's infatuation with Coppinger, but, after careful thought, he decides that he must take the initiative. "Doubt," the author says, "is at once the wisdom and the weakness of the reflective man" (220). Leo's musings force him to admit to himself that Magdalena probably married him to escape the oppressive role that a Mexican husband would have imposed on her. Their relationship, he realizes, has always been that of father and daughter; and, now that she has finally grown up, she loves him but not as a husband. Her true destiny, he painfully concedes, lies with Coppinger. Leo knows that, since his marriage was never sanctioned by the Church, it can be easily annulled, leaving Magdalena free of legal obligation. When his friend Padre Orlando agrees to make arrangements for such an action, Leo immediately leaves the town, the scene of his great victory, and rides alone into the desert night: "After the agony of human contact, the ordeal of love and friendship, the prickly tangle of pain and confusion in which he had lived for weeks, this unpeopled quiet seemed a welcome refuge, and so did the weariness that promised oblivion" (250).

With this expression of spiritual exhaustion, the story of Leo Mendes ends. But does it? Daniel Larid in *Grant of Kingdom* utters a similar wish to retreat from the teeming world of man's making; but such, Fergusson implies, can never be the active man's fate. Renewed and refreshed, Laird returns from the mountains to make a name for himself. Other of Fergusson's characters dream (as does Morgan Riley, for example, in *The Life of Riley*) of "retiring to some beautiful wilderness where desire might peacefully subside and money seem unimportant" (204). But, except for the chronic idlers, the author's people understand that these longings will never be realized—are regressive fantasies not to be seriously entertained. In Leo's case, the reader, of course, recalls Delores Pino's prophecy that "You are a man of many lives." Leo's own belief that, "When a way and a phase of life is over, the man who lived it dies and must be reborn" (212) no doubt foretells his future.

Toward the end of the novel, Leo, on a visit to Santa Fe, thinks of returning to northern New Mexico, where the coming of the railroad is rapidly transforming the area's slow-moving society; to survive, Leo admits, he must somehow reconcile himself to a changing world. Specifically, his future is perhaps foreshadowed by the offer of a job (an event which also occurs near the close of the book) as the Eastern buyer for a large Santa Fe merchandising firm. But, whatever course he chooses to follow, we cannot believe that Leo, in his own way as vital and vibrant as any of the writer's previous heroes, will be satisfied for very long apart from the competitive struggle which, in Fergusson's scheme of things, is such a necessary ingredient in the experience of living. Leo is, by his very nature, a "conqueror"; the possibility that he might become a "drifter"—in the manner of Morgan Riley—is inconceivable.

The Conquest of Don Pedro was probably, from a financial standpoint, the author's most successful book. It was a 1954 selection by the Literary Guild, and a special edition of the novel was published for members of the book club; and, in addition, the work enjoyed good sales as a paperback. Moreover, the novel was well received by reviewers. Dan Wickenden, in a page-one review of the novel in the *New York Herald Tribune Book Review*, wrote: "In his fine, clear prose, Harvey Fergusson has carved from the raw material of the Southwest a notable work of art. . . . With *The Conquest of Don Pedro*, the fourteenth of his published works, one of America's finest writers comes triumphantly into his own."[8] Wickenden's praise is high but, I believe, deserved. *The Conquest of Don Pedro* is without question one of the best American novels of the post-World War II period—and one of the least known. Its technical achievements—balanced and rounded structure, limpid style, characters who are vivid and alive—have not been surpassed, and seldom equaled, by American novelists of the last quarter-century.

But technical perfection in itself does not make a novel great, and the special power of *The Conquest of Don Pedro* derives principally, I think, from the character of Leo Mendes. The book, as James K. Folsom suggests, is "more psychologically oriented than the earlier novels."[9] Certainly Fergusson in this narrative is more interested than he had been in previous stories in following the mental processes of his central character, and most of the book's dramatic situations clearly issue from Leo's remarkable mind. Viewed in the abstract, Leo's life and attitudes illustrate, as do those of Fergusson's earlier characters, the author's theories of motivation and behavior. But rather than simply stating that something happens, Fergusson demonstrates how Leo's long and sometimes painful reflections are the source of his actions; and he does so with sympathy and an understanding of Leo's complex nature. The result, surely, is that Leo Mendes is Fergusson's most attractive and believable character, a man drawn from the writer's rich store of thought and experience.

Though different in many ways, *Grant of Kingdom* and *The Conquest of Don Pedro* are, taken together, the satisfying fruition of the author's genius. Coming at the conclusion of a long career, these exceptional books (like all his previous ones) dramatize the writer's vision of life—but the vision is now softened and humanized by the gifts of wisdom and sympathy, gifts bestowed only by the passage of time. These works somehow capture the physical and emotional vitality of the Western pioneer, and they comprehend at the same time the desires of his heart as well as the fact of his courage. In them, Fergusson's technical skill, combined with his generous insight into the mysteries of human conduct, fashioned a pair of novels that any writer would be proud to claim.

CHAPTER 8

Literary Theory and Accomplishment

I have not, to this point, spoken of Fergusson's literary philosophy because I believe that the writer's books should be allowed to speak for themselves on this subject. Moreover, it is entirely possible that the author himself never attempted to formulate an explicit and coherent theory of art; certainly he never, during his lifetime, reduced such a theory to print. In the writing of his books, he seemed much more interested in illustrating points of social and personal philosophy than in experimenting with technique on the one hand or adhering to strict principles of composition on the other.

In most aspects of fiction-writing (an exception is plot development, an area in which he consistently had difficulty), Fergusson was an impeccable technician; but he was not, as I have already observed, inclined toward experiment or innovation. In his novels, the narrative is usually traditional in point of view and in structure, and is always straightforwardly developed. Perhaps the most striking technical aspect of the writer's fiction is a limpid and subtly rhythmic style, one which is serviceable and eminently readable and obviously the product of long and devoted toil. His language, however, though polished and sometimes even glittering, contains few premeditated effects or mannerisms that would stamp it as his individualized creation. For this author, then, the intellectual and narrative content of his works was his primary concern; techniques of presentation were decidedly secondary considerations.

Still, it is reasonable to assume that Fergusson, as is no doubt true of any serious writer, possessed a set of working principles

139

and beliefs which, if they can be briefly summarized, may reveal
something of his unarticulated theory as a literary artist. These
principles must be pieced together from several sources; but,
with the author's fourteen books as background, a few comments
and speculations about them may be helpful in understanding
more thoroughly Fergusson's objectives as a writer.

I   The Writer's Credo

In *Home in the West,* Fergusson enumerates the circumstances
in his early life that pointed him in the direction of a literary
career; but he says little concerning his philosophy of art. In that
work, for instance, he tells us that his childhood training in
sketching and drawing taught him to observe the world accurately
and in detail—for a writer, certainly, an invaluable ability. His
anti-social impulses as an adolescent, he contends, created in
him the capacity for viewing mankind and all his works with a
curious but detached and sometimes disbelieving eye. This early
skepticism and sense of separation perhaps explain in part the
writer's tendency, noted previously, to keep a discreet distance
between himself and most of his characters. He also provides in
Home in the West a brief account of his protracted struggle to
chasten an unruly language—an effort which, as already indicated, resulted eventually in a style of admirable clarity and precision.

In reconstructing an author's literary credo, the student can
sometimes extract useful clues from the writings of those who
have influenced that author. Fergusson admitted to no special
and abiding influences on his work; but he did, in various places,
list many writers whose books he had read and studied—and presumably emulated in some way. In *Home in the West,* he mentions nature and adventure writers (such as Thoreau, Kipling, and
Conrad) and prophets of intellectual rebellion (such as H. L.
Mencken and Van Wyck Brooks) as having been his most memorable reading fare as a child and adolescent. In an autobiographical
note supplied to Charles C. Baldwin in 1924—and included in
the latter's *The Men Who Make Our Novels*—Fergusson says the
following: "I had a period of Bernard Shaw and Ibsen, and
another when decadents like Wilde, Hearn and Gautier were my
models. But the novelists that influenced me most, in about the

order named, were Maupassant, Turgenieff, Tolstoy, Flaubert, George Moore and Thomas Hardy. I never found anything I liked in American fiction except *Huckleberry Finn* and a few of my contemporaries, who came too late to influence me." He had recently been reading, he continues, a great deal in the literature of psychoanalysis. He concludes: "I cannot, however, lay claim to a finished method of the novel. . . . Most aesthetic theory seems to me ridiculous."[1]

Probably the author's most revealing comments on art and literature appear in an extended passage from *Modern Man*. His reasons for placing the passage in that particular book never become altogether clear, but Fergusson seems to imply that the principles of mental and emotional equilibrium (or lack of it) developed in *Modern Man* are as valid for judging art and the artist as they are for considering other segments of society. For instance, he cites the neo-Catholic movement among many intellectuals of the 1920's and 1930's as a splendid example of regressive behavior—an effort to "crawl back into the womb of the cultural past" (144). Moreover, he isolates D. H. Lawrence, "a man of great poetic insight" (144), as representative of the typical twentieth-century neurotic who is given to excessive indulgence in fantasy and in desires to return to the past. Lawrence's "religion that blood and flesh are wiser than intellect and are always right" (145), Fergusson contends, could never be accepted by any rational individual capable of functioning in the real modern world.

As Fergusson makes abundantly clear in *Modern Man*, his own literary theory and practice differ radically from the popular modes of expression that various cults of twentieth-century writers have propagated. In particular, he despises the artist or intellectual whose only interest is himself. "This kind of writer, in the first place," he says,

almost always takes himself as his principal subject, most of his other characters being seen merely as a part of his environment. In the second place, his writing lacks both movement in itself and the power to suggest movement in his symbols and figures. He deals in relationships and states of mind rather than events and gets his effects by cumulation and contrast rather than by movement and development. As a corollary of this, his work is usually pedantic—that is, it exploits a vast erudition, for its own sake, and seeks always in some measure to make literature out of other literature by a variety of recombinations, allusions, parodies, and imitations. Lastly, both his style and his vision are always more or less disintegrate. (150–51)

The works of this type of intellectual, Fergusson asserts, represent the unhealthy tendency in recent times to separate imaginative and creative thought from the practical act of living. He mentions Marcel Proust, James Joyce, and T. S. Eliot as prominent examples of the kind of writer he describes. Joyce, in particular, offers Fergusson what he regards as an especially unfortunate case. Joyce, the author believes, had extraordinary talents; he experimented boldly and thereby contributed to the stock of techniques that other writers have to work with. Still, he fell into the trap of becoming a subjective intellectual with the result that his works, from the early short stories to *Finnegan's Wake,* exhibit a "progressive decline into obscurity" (153). The objective artist, on the other hand—and Fergusson obviously considers himself a representative of this type—"almost always shows a gain in clarity as his symbols become more fully realized and the integration of his works more complete" (153).

In *Modern Man,* Fergusson also voices dismay about the modern writer's eagerness to indulge in free-wheeling linguistic experiments. Language, he contends, "is a means of communication, and all its usefulness as such depends upon some agreement as to the meaning of its symbols, and upon a commonly accepted logic in their arrangement, so that the disintegrative process cannot go far without defeating the only conceivable use of writing at all" (158).

Fergusson is also contemptuous of those literary pursuits that are directly dependent on the creative artist's labors. Of scholarship he says: "This tendency to accumulation for the sake of accumulation, and without regard to use, is an invariable symptom of impotence. Men gather things when they can no longer do things" (157). Nor does he have much respect for broader kinds of literary criticism. In this regard, we might observe that Fergusson's own excursions into criticism—if his sweeping generalizations in *Modern Man* can be labeled as such—scarcely serve to advance the critical arts' reputation for detached evaluation. Like Edgar Allan Poe's, Fergusson's comments on literature tend to be extrapolations of personal practices into general theory. I do not mean to imply, of course, that his judgments are wholly without value; he is correct, for instance, in asserting that the landscape of recent American and European fiction is littered with the disembodied shapes of stricken psyches (though whether this circumstance is good or bad for modern fiction seems to remain a matter for individual evaluation). Unquestionably, however, Fergusson's judgments derive from a rather narrow and individual view of art, rather than from wide and analytical reading.

Though Fergusson's remarks in *Modern Man* are mostly negative, it is easy enough, by reversal and inference, to discern the outlines of his positive literary theory. He believed, for example, that the artist's method should be inductive rather than deductive. He affirmed that the writer's task is to observe objects rather than to explore interior patterns. "When the artist," Fergusson writes in *Modern Man,* "projects his emotion into a symbol—a character who is not himself—he necessarily leaves out everything that is particular and peculiar to himself. He must do this in order to make the character credible. What the character therefore embodies is those qualities of the experience expressed which are universally human, rather than those peculiar to the artist" (155). Subjectivity, Fergusson continues, inevitably issues into peculiarity, obscurity, and queerness; but objectivity leads the artist to a discovery of universal principles. From this premise, it is a simple matter to understand Fergusson's preference in his own fiction for the broad social canvas which features both clear outlines and attention to detail. It is also easy to see why much of his fiction is intended to illustrate a predictable pattern of beliefs and assumptions which the author conceived to be universal standards of human behavior.

II Final Assessment

At present it is safe to say, I think, that the bulk of Fergusson's reputation rests on his talents as a writer of fiction; and, as a novelist, two general terms seem best to describe him: he was a philosophical novelist, and he was a novelist of manners. He was a philosophical novelist because he developed a coherent and consistent system of beliefs, both practical and metaphysical, and then designed a series of characters and incidents to illustrate those beliefs. This technique—the rationale for which, as we have

seen, is provided in *Modern Man*—is the weakest and most controversial aspect of Fergusson's art. A writer, of course, must
begin with certain working assumptions concerning man and the
universe, and more specifically concerning human thought and
action; but, if he is honest, the writer readily admits that people
are so various and so unpredictable that no one theory comprehends the full range of their behavior. Fergusson, however,
was insistent in contending that his set of premises is not only
valid but precise enough to forecast the ultimate fate of his
characters.

Far from being the open and detached observer of human behavior that he claimed he was, Fergusson viewed his characters'
actions through a veil of preconceptions; and he judged them as
human beings in terms of how completely they lived up to those
preconceptions. Perhaps Fergusson's system, at its inception, derived largely from practical experience and observation; it was
formulated, however, rather early in his career; and, though it
was modified on occasion, it remained essentially unchanged for
half a century. Such inflexibility, it seems to me, is unworthy of a
thinker as fertile and inventive as Fergusson sometimes showed
himself to be.

In any event, Fergusson's theory of behavior—which, whether
stated or not, is the continuous backdrop of his fiction—gives rise
to two unfortunate side effects. First, it creates in the reader an
uncomfortable feeling that the author's characters are moving, not
independently and spontaneously, but according to the dictates of
a backstage director. Needless to say, this is not true of all
Fergusson's characters—several of them, as I have tried to dem-
onstrate, are superlatively realistic people who grow in the
reader's mind and enjoy a life not bounded by the author's
theories—but it mars enough of them so as to be a significant feature of his writings. Second, the reader sometimes finds himself
privately quarreling with the writer's premises and assumptions
and is thus distracted from following a book's particular line of
development. Even if, on the whole, he agrees with the author's
beliefs, such a reader is likely to find many minor theoretical
points to which he takes exception. Such belligerent reactions
most often occur in connection with the nonfiction, but they occasionally interrupt the reading of even the best novels.

But, if Fergusson was in large measure ineffective as a

philosophical novelist, his novels of manners more than compensate for failings in the former category. Since the label "novelist of manners" is usually applied to English Victorians such as Thackeray and Trollope, some readers may be mildly shocked that I have used it to describe a Western American writer like Fergusson. The stereotyped image of the Southwest as a land of wild and woolly creatures, both men and animals, has probably caused many people to conclude that the region had—and has—no manners. But even in the strictest meaning of that term ("social conduct," according to the dictionary, "or rules of conduct as shown in prevalent customs"), many groups within the area—the Spanish-Americans, for example—have cultivated highly distinctive manners (and often very elaborate and courtly ones). In the more general sense of the word, the Southwest has also developed a recognizable society, which, while rudimentary perhaps, is not unlike the larger society of which it is a part. Through reading and direct experience, Fergusson studied the region's manners in detail and in general pattern; and many of his novels are loving and minute recreations of these social customs from their earliest recorded appearance in the Southwest to their present-day manifestations.

As Fergusson's remarks in *Modern Man* concerning the objective versus the subjective artist make plain, his theory of art—to the extent that he formulated one—was really a version of nineteenth-century Realism (with perhaps a tip of the cap to the determinist philosophies of Naturalism). William Dean Howells said that the Realistic novel should be a "study of individual traits and general conditions as they make themselves known to American experience,"[2] and the Realists generally believed that the true meaning of existence is found in the everyday life, both personal and social, of the typical citizen—the proverbial "slice of life" cut from the loaf of ordinary society. That the typical citizen of the nineteenth-century Southwest—a mountain man or a Spanish don or an Indian warrior—may seem to most Americans a rather exotic creature does not diminish his representativeness within a regional context; and certainly Fergusson usually selected for his protagonist in a novel a representative, rather than a singular, character.

Moreover, the author normally eschewed the sensational events that are the staple of much Western fiction; he preferred instead to trace an ordinary individual's movements through the expanding web of a formative society. Since he claimed only the most superficial personal identification with his characters, Fergusson, unlike most twentieth-century novelists, did not attempt deeply or subtly to probe his people's emotions or motivations —the lone exception here being the character of Leo Mendes in *The Conquest of Don Pedro*—nor was he interested in exploring their subjective states of consciousness. On the contrary, he was much more concerned with following the surface pattern of their relationships with their fellow men; and, since his ability to accomplish this task was well-developed and gifted, his inclination was a fortunate one. In his novels, then, Fergusson is most forceful when he is at work gauging the mass and density, the manners and nuances, of almost any social situation. And he so did with consummate and flawless skill; I venture to suggest, in fact, that he was one of the most accomplished writers in the Realistic vein (using "Realism" here to designate a commonly accepted approach to fiction-writing) that America has so far produced.

Defining "success" is, under ideal conditions, a tricky business; and certain facets of Fergusson's career make the term, as a measure of achievement, more than ordinarily slippery. Perhaps, then, there is little need to speculate on whether or not Fergusson as a writer was personally and professionally "successful," but some brief comment on the subject seems in order at this point. Certainly his works have won for him a growing number of admirers and, during his lifetime, at least a taste of literary fame. The books usually enjoyed favorable reviews upon publication —some of them elicited lavish praise from reviewers[3]—and they generally sold well. The list of writers, critics, and scholars who have commented favorably on his works is impressive: H. L. Mencken, Charles C. Baldwin, Floyd Dell, J. Frank Dobie, T. K. Whipple, Lawrence Clark Powell, James K. Folsom, and Cecil Robinson, to name a few. Still, despite these and other examples of deserved praise, it seems clear that Fergusson's books at this juncture in time have not received the recognition, either in the writer's native West or in the country as a whole, that they genuinely merit.

The reasons for their humble status in the rankings of most critics of American literature should be obvious. The author himself once commented—in a symposium on the Western novel conducted by John R. Milton in the Autumn, 1964, issue of *The South Dakota Review*—on the failure of Eastern readers and critics to recognize the achievements of major Western writers. That failure, Fergusson contended, is the result of the pernicious effects of the popular "cowboy romance," which has "deteriorated over the years into a stereotyped fable with stereotyped characters. . . . The mere word Western alienates a horde of readers. Also, most American reviewers and critics live in New York, care nothing about the West and know nothing about it except that any novel dealing with 'the great open spaces' must be treated with a certain condescension."[4] Added to this widespread prejudice is the fact that Fergusson, as explained above, was a kind of throwback to nineteenth-century Realism and therefore did not benefit from the publicity accorded more fashionable modes of literary expression. Because his novels are in no way sensational or formally experimental, they receive none of the irrelevant attention that is showered on the works of more daring writers. To most commentators, then, viewing them from the perspective of the Eastern seaboard, Fergusson's novels must seem rather plain and simple.

The reasons, on the other hand, that Fergusson, even in his native region, was sometimes misunderstood and his works discounted are not so easily discerned. James K. Folsom is probably right in contending that Fergusson was "a prophet without honor in his own literary country . . . because his fictional values are totally opposite to those of most of the region's authors."[5] Professor Max Westbrook—in a celebrated essay which appeared in *Western American Literature*, a journal sponsored by the Western Literature Association—asserts that the most prominent characteristic of the Western writer is a belief in "sacrality": "a belief in God as energy. . . . The emphasis is placed on energy as *primary*, as a power more fundamental than ethics or the intellect."[6] Westbrook then lists several common traits which spring from this initial premise.[7] Stripped of its rather complicated diction, this argument is basically that the typical Western writer is a Romantic in something like the traditional literary meaning of that term.[8]

But Fergusson, on the contrary, though he accepted a limited version of what might be called "unconscious intuition" and though he affirmed the near-mystical powers inherent in nature, was not in any meaningful sense a Romantic. While many Western writers, for example, are anti-rational and aspire to the "blood consciousness" espoused by D. H. Lawrence, Fergusson calmly upheld the efficacy of human reason and technological progress. While many of Western literature's most cherished works seem little more than tracts in a back-to-nature movement, Fergusson questioned the value of the natural life and championed large cities as the true strongholds of individual liberty. While the central figure of many Western novels is the heroic loner who flees from the encroachments of organized society, Fergusson in his fiction attempted to show the disastrous consequences of a character's failure to accommodate himself to the social order. And, while much Western writing is notoriously committed to a simplified and attractive view of history, Fergusson approached the past gingerly and warned of its dangers when an individual uses it as a retreat from the chaotic present. Demonstrably, then, the author's beliefs concerning man and society ran almost directly counter to those of his Western colleagues. And despite the fact that his best works are easily the equal of those of such Western writers as Walter Van Tilburg Clark, Vardis Fisher, Frederick Manfred, Frank Waters, and Wright Morris, they are suffered, in some quarters within the region, only with a large measure of distrust and alarm. Thus does suspicion, I think, breed unjust neglect.

Fergusson himself, apparently, was never very hopeful concerning his future position in literary history. "I write a book," he said in *Home in the West*, "because I must, not because I expect success. Anything that looks like triumph I regard with skeptical surprise. A lack of confidence in one's own success is a serious handicap, and I have experienced it to the full . . ." (138). For the craftsman, he continued, a job well done is its own reward. Still, a modicum of praise can be a balm to the spirit, and it would have been a modest and not unbecoming ambition were the author to have hoped merely for a proper ranking on the scale of twentieth-century American novelists. I will not attempt, in conclusion, to promote Fergusson as a major American literary figure; that would be unfair to both the man and his works. Nor do I claim that it is either possible or desirable that the reader assent fully to Fergusson's theories of human behavior—or even perhaps to his views on Southwestern history and society. But he was, I believe, a very good writer and one worthy of serious study. He was a disciplined stylist and provocative thinker whose books may stir controversy but are never dull. They amply repay—in entertainment, in broad knowledge, and in mental stimulation—all who consult them. And they will soon be adjudged, I trust, for what they are: genuine contributions to the literature of the West and to American literature generally. I agree with Saul Cohen, who predicts that "the day is not far off when Fergusson will be 'discovered,' and the work of an important American writer will receive deserving but overdue recognition."[9]

Notes and References

Preface

1. Cecil Robinson, "Legend of Destiny: The American Southwest in the Novels of Harvey Fergusson," *The American West*, IV (November, 1967): 17.
2. Lawrence Clark Powell, *Southwestern Book Trails: A Reader's Guide to the Heartland of New Mexico and Arizona* (Albuquerque, 1963), p. 19.

Chapter One

1. Powell, *Southwestern Book Trails*, p. 2.
2. Biographical information, except where noted, was obtained during a personal interview with Harvey Fergusson at his home in Berkeley, California, July 21, 1968.
3. *Home in the West: An Inquiry into My Origins* (New York, 1944), p. 21.
4. *Ibid.*, p. 35.
5. *Ibid.*, p. 47.
6. *Ibid.*, p. 68.
7. Harvey Butler Fergusson, "The Making of a Constitution" (address delivered September 19, 1910, at the University of New Mexico), *Bulletin of the University of New Mexico*, I (October, 1910): 11.
8. "Conversation with Harvey Fergusson," edited by John R. Milton, *South Dakota Review*, IX (Spring, 1971): 39.
9. See Virginia Gillespie, "This Old House," *New Mexico Magazine*, XLV (February, 1967): 2–5.
10. *Home in the West*, p. 74.
11. *Ibid.*, p. 78.
12. Lina Fergusson Browne, ed., *J. Ross Browne: His Letters, Journals and Writings* (Albuquerque, 1969).
13. For a valuable collection of interviews with Fergusson's childhood

playmates and acquaintances, see John Cleveland Baker, "Autobiographical Elements in the Works of Harvey Fergusson," unpublished Master's thesis (University of Texas, 1940).

14. *Home in the West*, p. 119.

15. *Ibid.*

16. *Ibid.*, p. 192.

17. *Ibid.*, pp. 227–28.

18. Charles W. Ferguson, "Harvey Fergusson Declares a Writer Must Leave His Native Environment," *Dallas Morning News*, September 5, 1926, p. 16.

19. *Home in the West*, p. 120.

20. "Albuquerque Revisited: A Preface to the Apollo Edition of *Rio Grande*," *Rio Grande* (New York, 1955), p. xi.

21. *Home in the West*, p. 236.

22. *Ibid.*, p. 20.

23. *Ibid.*, p. 74.

24. Charles C. Baldwin, *The Men Who Make Our Novels* (New York, 1924), p. 154.

25. Rebecca McCann, *The Complete Cheerful Cherub*, with a memoir by Mary Graham Bonner (New York, 1932), p. 12.

26. A quotation from Howard Raper, a boyhood friend of Fergusson's. See Baker, p. 48.

27. Personal letter from Fergusson, August 22, 1967.

28. Statement made by Fergusson to W. T. Pilkington during personal interview, July 21, 1968.

Chapter Two

1. *Modern Man: His Belief and Behavior* (New York, 1936), p. viii. Subsequent page references to the book are given in the text in parentheses.

2. Interestingly, though he read Thoreau enthusiastically as a child, Fergusson appears in *Modern Man* to have rejected much of Thoreau's philosophy, especially the doctrines of living simply and outside the social mechanism.

3. See, for example, some of the statements in "Modern Man and Harvey Fergusson—A Symposium," *New Mexico Quarterly*, VI (May, 1936): 123–35.

4. A convenient summary of these criticisms is R. H. Waters's untitled review of *Modern Man*, which appeared in *American Journal of Psychology*, XLVIII (October, 1936): 701–02.

5. E. T. Hiller, untitled review of *Modern Man*, *American Sociological Review*, I (April, 1936): 321.

6. *People and Power: A Study of Political Behavior in America* (New

York, 1947), p. 25. Subsequent page references to the book are given in the text in parentheses.

Chapter Three

1. *Capitol Hill: A Novel of Washington Life* (New York, 1923), p. 3. Subsequent page references to the novel are given in the text in parentheses.

2. Quoted from an advertisement at the end of *Women and Wives* (New York, 1924).

3. James K. Folsom, *Harvey Fergusson,* (Austin, Texas; 1969), p. 39.

4. *Women and Wives,* p. 24. Subsequent page references to the novel are given in the text in parentheses.

5. Lorene Pearson, "Harvey Fergusson and the Crossroads," *New Mexico Quarterly,* XXI (Autumn, 1951): 340–41; see also Folsom, pp. 23–24.

Chapter Four

1. *Home in the West,* p. v. Subsequent page references to the book are given in the text in parentheses.

2. Wallace Stegner, "Born a Square: The Westerner's Dilemma," *Atlantic Monthly,* CCXIII (January, 1964): 46–50.

3. Quoted by Lawrence Clark Powell in *Books West Southwest* (Los Angeles, 1957), p. 24.

4. See, for example, the anonymous and untitled review of *Home in the West* in *Catholic World,* CLXI (June, 1945): 284–85; see also Russell Maloney, "Fergusson on Fergusson," *The New Yorker,* XX (January 27, 1945): 61–63. Both reviewers—along with several writing in other publications—severely criticize Fergusson for dwelling at such length on his personal sexual history since any such individual history is, by itself, supposedly trivial and insignificant. In the book, however, the author clearly demonstrates how his personal experiences relate to the work's overall thematic concerns. *Home in the West,* if I may judge by the reviews of it, has been the most misread and misunderstood of Fergusson's books.

5. Erna Fergusson, *Our Southwest* (New York, 1940), p. 375.

6. Cecil Robinson, *With the Ears of Strangers: The Mexican in American Literature* (Tucson, 1963), p. 75.

7. *The Blood of the Conquerors* (New York, 1921), p. 16. Subsequent page references to the novel are given in the text in parentheses.

8. Pearson, p. 338.

9. *Hot Saturday* (New York, 1926), p. 40. Subsequent page references to the novel are given in the text in parentheses.

10. Folsom, p. 26.

11. Pearson, pp. 344–45.

Chapter Five

1. *Footloose McGarnigal* (New York, 1930), p. 3. Subsequent page references to the novel are given in the text in parentheses.

2. Fergusson summarized his attitudes toward such people in an article called "The Cult of the Indian," *Scribner's Magazine*, LXXXVIII (August, 1930): 129–33.

3. See Leo Marx, *The Machine in the Garden: Technology and the Pastoral Ideal in America* (New York, 1964), pp. 16–19.

4. See, for example, Folsom, p. 26; see also Pearson, p. 345.

5. *The Life of Riley* (New York, 1937), p. 38. Subsequent page references to the novel are given in the text in parentheses.

6. Pearson, p. 350.

Chapter Six

1. "Introduction," *Followers of the Sun: A Trilogy of the Santa Fe Trail* (New York, 1936), p. ix.

2. *Ibid.*, p. x.

3. *Ibid.*, pp. v–vi.

4. *Ibid.*, p. vi.

5. "Introduction," *The Last Rustler: The Autobiography of Lee Sage* (Boston, 1930), p. viii.

6. *Ibid.*, p. v.

7. Erna Fergusson, p. 375.

8. Powell, *Books West Southwest*, p. 33.

9. J. Frank Dobie, *The Mustangs* (Boston, 1952), p. xii.

10. *Rio Grande* (New York, 1933), p. xvii. Subsequent page references to the book are given in the text in parentheses.

11. Ross Calvin, *Sky Determines: An Interpretation of the Southwest*, rev. ed. (Albuquerque, 1965), p. ix.

12. Pearson, p. 349.

13. *Wolf Song* (New York, 1927), p. 12. Subsequent page references to the novel are given in the text in parentheses.

14. Robinson, *With the Ears of Strangers*, p. 84.

15. The author's indebtedness to Ruxton is detailed by Bonnie Reading Thrift in her unpublished Master's thesis, "Harvey Fergusson's Use of Southwest History and Customs in His Novels" (University of Texas, 1940).

16. George Frederick Ruxton, *In the Old West*, ed. Horace Kephart (New York, 1915), pp. 295–301.

17. "Introduction," *Followers of the Sun*, pp. x–xi.

18. J. Frank Dobie, "Earth and Metal," *Southwest Review*, XXXV (Autumn, 1950), p. xix.

19. "Introduction," *Followers of the Sun*, p. xi.

20. *In Those Days: An Impression of Change* (New York, 1929), p. 6. Subsequent page references to the novel are given in the text in parentheses.

21. Folsom, p. 16.

Chapter Seven

1. Though Fergusson's magazine stories of the 1920's were obviously examples of the author's "pandering to popular tastes," Fergusson himself had no illusions concerning the literary status of these tales. He wrote them to make money, did not himself take them seriously, and certainly did not expect readers to take them seriously. They were "hack work," he once said, written "in order to make a living." (Quotation is from a personal letter from Fergusson, dated July 10, 1968.)

2. *Grant of Kingdom* (New York, 1950), p. v. Subsequent page references to the novel are given in the text in parentheses.

3. See especially Robinson, "Legend of Destiny," pp. 16–17.

4. *Ibid.*, p. 68.

5. Pearson, p. 352.

6. Dobie, "Earth and Metal," p. xx.

7. *The Conquest of Don Pedro* (New York, 1954), p. 3. Subsequent page references to the novel are given in the text in parentheses.

8. Dan Wickenden, "Long Ago, and Far Away," *New York Herald Tribune Book Review*, June 27, 1954, p. 1.

9. Folsom, p. 37.

Chapter Eight

1. Baldwin, pp. 164–65.

2. William Dean Howells, *Criticism and Fiction* (New York, 1891), Chapter XXI.

3. The plaudits of book reviewers, however, must be probed with a skeptical eye. Saul Cohen, in the unpublished text of a speech on Fergusson and his works, delivered before the Zamorano Book Club of Los Angeles in March, 1968, carefully lists and compares the reviews which greeted each of the author's novels. According to Cohen, an interesting pattern emerges from these notices. The reviewers seem to concur, he says, on the proposition that "Fergusson writes well." They also agree that "Fergusson can tell a story; but this is in our day often to damn with faint praise. It is the comment one makes about Somerset Maugham be-

fore proceeding to tear his work apart." Certainly the technique, common among some reviewers, of transforming a writer's virtues into implied criticisms was used on Fergusson on more than one occasion. Mr. Cohen, incidentally, generously supplied me a typescript copy of his talk.

4. "The Western Novel—A Symposium," edited by John R. Milton, *South Dakota Review*, II (Autumn, 1964): 24.

5. Folsom, p. 40.

6. Max Westbrook, "The Practical Spirit: Sacrality and the American West," *Western American Literature*, III (Fall, 1968): 198.

7. Westbrook summarizes these subsidiary traits most succinctly in his book, *Walter Van Tilburg Clark* (New York, 1969), p. 46:

First . . . for the sacred man of the American West, it is presumptuous to think an individual's intellect can formulate the infinite. Second, the end hoped for is not a state achieved but an attitude—felt but never owned—toward a reality which touches but which is never confined by the intellect. Third, what is commonly called evil is an intellectual confusion of forces which are an intrinsic part of man and nature. . . . These forces—brute drives, if you will, but not evil—can be appeased, shaped away from destructive action, only through the individual's courage to be human, to listen to those archetypal meanings which are given voice through the unconscious. Fourth, the Christian God is a concoction of the rational mind, an illusion of man's desire to have a comforting and personal attention from on high. . . . Fifth, the hope of man is to establish contact with the original, the source, to "start with the sun."

8. Richard P. Adams's recent definition of American Romanticism, in fact, sounds remarkably similar to Westbrook's concept of Western "sacrality." See Adams's "Permutations of American Romanticism," *Studies in Romanticism*, IX (Fall, 1970): 249–68.

9. Saul Cohen, *Harvey Fergusson: A Checklist* (Los Angeles, 1965), p. 1.

Selected Bibliography

PRIMARY SOURCES

Works by Harvey Fergusson are listed according to the order in which they were published. All known American editions of the books are cited; translations and foreign editions have been omitted.

A. *Books*

The Blood of the Conquerors. New York: Alfred A. Knopf, 1921. New York: Alfred A. Knopf, 1921 (Borzoi Pocket Book edition). New York: Modern Age Books, 1937.

Capitol Hill: A Novel of Washington Life. New York: Alfred A. Knopf, 1923. New York: Alfred A. Knopf, 1926 (Borzoi Pocket Book edition).

Women and Wives. New York: Alfred A. Knopf, 1924. New York: Alfred A. Knopf, 1927 (Borzoi Pocket Book edition).

Hot Saturday. New York: Alfred A. Knopf, 1926. Concord, New Hampshire: American Mercury, 1926 (Mercury Book edition).

Wolf Song. New York: Alfred A. Knopf, 1927. New York: Grosset and Dunlap, n. d. New York: Bantam Books, 1951 (paperback).

In Those Days: An Impression of Change. New York: Alfred A. Knopf, 1929. New York: Bantam Books, 1951 (paperback).

Footloose McGarnigal. New York: Alfred A. Knopf, 1930.

Rio Grande. New York: Alfred A. Knopf, 1933. New York: Tudor Publishing Company, 1945. New York: William Morrow and Company, 1955. New York: Apollo Editions, n. d. (paperback).

Modern Man: His Belief and Behavior. New York: Alfred A. Knopf, 1936.

Followers of the Sun: A Trilogy of the Santa Fe Trail. (Contains *The Blood of the Conquerors*, *Wolf Song*, and *In Those Days*.) New York: Alfred A. Knopf, 1936. New York: Grosset and Dunlap, n.d. (published under the title *The Santa Fe Omnibus*).

The Life of Riley. New York: Alfred A. Knopf, 1937. New York: Grosset and Dunlap, n. d. New York: Bantam Books, 1952 (paperback, published under the title *What a Man Wants*).

Home in the West: An Inquiry into My Origins. New York: Duell, Sloan and Pearce, 1944.

People and Power: A Study of Political Behavior in America. New York: William Morrow and Company, 1947.

Grant of Kingdom. New York: William Morrow and Company, 1950. New York: Pocket Books, 1952 (paperback).

The Conquest of Don Pedro. New York: William Morrow and Company, 1954. New York: William Morrow and Company, 1954 (Literary Guild book club edition). New York: Pocket Books, 1955 (paperback). Albuquerque: University of New Mexico Press, 1974 (paperback).

B. *Shorter Works*

The following is a selected listing, arranged chronologically according to date of publication; much of the author's newspaper writing and magazine fiction is either currently inaccessible or of no interest to the student of literature.

"How the Government Is Governed," *New York Times*, May 20, 1923, Section 4, p. 5.

"The Washington Job-Holder," *The American Mercury*, I (March, 1924): 345–50.

"Billy the Kid," *The American Mercury*, V (June, 1925): 224–31.

"Out Where the Bureaucracy Begins," *The Nation*, CXXI (July 22, 1925): 112–14.

"The New Englander" (short story), *The American Mercury*, VII (February, 1926): 187–95.

"The Cult of the Indian," *Scribner's Magazine*, LXXXVIII (August, 1930): 129–33.

"Foreword" (pp. vii–viii) to *The Last Rustler: The Autobiography of Lee Sage*. Boston: Little, Brown, 1930.

"Exploring the Southwest in Your Own Motor," *Travel*, LVI (October, 1931): 26–28, 48.

"Introduction" (pp. ix–xi) to *El Gringo, or New Mexico and Her People* by W. W. H. Davis. Santa Fe: Rydal Press, 1938.

"Timber Line" (poem), *New Mexico Magazine*, XXXV (July, 1957): 28.

"The Western Novel—A Symposium: Harvey Fergusson" (ed. John R. Milton), *South Dakota Review*, II (Autumn, 1964): 23–24.

"Conversation with Harvey Ferguson" (ed. John R. Milton), *South Dakota Review*, IX (Spring, 1971): 39–45.

"Taos Remembered: Recollections of a Time of Innocence," *The American West*, VII (September, 1971): 38–41.

SECONDARY SOURCES

ANDERSON, MAXWELL. "Rio Grande," *The Nation*, CXXXVII (August 16, 1933): 190–91. Review of *Rio Grande*. Praises Fergusson's knowledge of the Southwestern past. Concludes that one reason for the book's "fascination is the perfection of the historical episode it rehearses. Here, in little, is an epitome of history."

AUSTIN, MARY. "Imaginative History," *Southwest Review*, XIX (Autumn, 1933): 19–21. Review of *Rio Grande*, by one of the Southwest's most celebrated writers. Judges the work as "perhaps the livest regional study that has yet appeared in America."

BALDWIN, CHARLES C. "Harvey Fergusson." *The Men Who Make Our Novels*. New York: Dodd, Mead, 1924. Brief critical evaluation of the author's first three novels. Asserts that, despite Fergusson's satirical and critical portraits of American society, "he has retained his faith in the vigor and hearty mirth and good clean earth that is America." Contains "a few autobiographic notes," which Fergusson "kindly jotted down . . . to make my account of him and his doings more complete."

BROUN, HEYWOOD. "A Group of Books Worth Reading," *The Bookman*, LIV (December, 1921): 393–97. Reviews, among other recently published novels, *The Blood of the Conquerors*. Calls it "a capital first novel," achieved by the "comparatively simple process" of the author's "keeping his eyes open." Likes every aspect of the book except the character of Julia Roth, who is merely "a lost doll in the middle of the desert."

COHEN, SAUL. *Harvey Fergusson: A Checklist* (leaflet). Los Angeles: University of California at Los Angeles Library, 1965. By far the best bibliography of Fergusson's published works. Should be used to supplement the listing provided here.

DELL, FLOYD. "Truthfuller Than Tolstoi (Harvey Fergusson)." *The Borzoi 1925*. New York: Alfred A. Knopf, 1925. Claims that Tolstoi occasionally lied about his characters "when he was bursting to prove some of his Manichean dogmas. . . . Harvey Fergusson, almost if not quite alone among the writers of our own day, never bothers with such lies. He simply has no pets." A fatuous argument; indicative, however, of Fergusson's high position among his colleagues of the 1920's.

DOBIE, J. FRANK. "Earth and Metal," *Southwest Review*, XXXV (Autumn, 1950): xviii–xxi. Reviews, with characteristic Dobie flair, *Grant of Kingdom*. Includes, in addition, comments on several of Fergusson's other books. Concludes that *Grant of Kingdom* is "competent, it is faithful to life and . . . it expresses prolonged understanding."

DUFFUS, R. L. "Modern Man and His Dilemmas," *New York Times Book Review*, January 26, 1936, p. 2. Highly favorable review of *Modern Man*. Contends that it is "one of the most civilized books of our rather uncivil period." Useful statement of a judgment of the work almost completely opposite to my own.

FOLSOM, JAMES K. *Harvey Fergusson*. Austin, Texas: Steck-Vaughn Company, 1969. (Pamphlet) Brief biography of the writer, followed by a survey of his writings. Generally perceptive; sometimes brilliant. Weakened by occasional lapses in style and organization.

HORGAN, PAUL. "New Mexico," *Yale Review*, XXIII (September, 1933): 211–13. Review of *Rio Grande*, by a popular Western novelist. Extremely sympathetic and laudatory comments. Believes the book is Fergusson's best to date.

JOHNSON, GERALD W. "Political Paradox of the Common Man," *New York Herald Tribune Weekly Book Review*, September 21, 1947, p. 2. Review of *People and Power*. Takes exception to several of the author's generalizations; offers a basically favorable judgment of the work, however.

KALLEN, H. M. "You Can't Win," *Saturday Review of Literature*, XIII (April 25, 1936): 12. Review of *Modern Man*. The reviewer, a professor of philosophy, acknowledges the book's "amateurism," a charge leveled by a number of professional psychologists, sociologists, and philosophers. Agrees with Fergusson's optimism concerning modern man's growth and potential.

KUNITZ, STANLEY J., and HOWARD HAYCRAFT. "Fergusson, Harvey." *Twentieth Century Authors*. New York: H. W. Wilson Company, 1942. Brief biographical sketch, much of it in the author's own words.

MALONEY, RUSSELL. "Fergusson on Fergusson," *The New Yorker*, XX (January 27, 1945): 61–63. Review of *Home in the West*. Typical of several reviews which wholly misunderstand the book. Argues that Fergusson probes every aspect of his background and environment except his own personality. Professes not to comprehend the reasons for the author's focus on his personal sexual attitudes. Generally snobbish and condescending.

McGINITY, SUE SIMMONS. "Harvey Fergusson's Use of Animal Imagery in Characterizing Spanish-American Women," *Western Review*, VIII (Winter, 1971): 46–50. Carefully documents a remarkably consistent pattern of "animalistic and primitive" metaphors employed by Fergusson to describe the "brown" women in his novels.

MENCKEN, H. L. "Essay in Pedagogy." *Prejudices: Fifth Series*. New York: Alfred A. Knopf, 1926. Extensive praise for *Capitol Hill*, probably the most "menckenesque" of Fergusson's books.

"Modern Man and Harvey Fergusson—A Symposium," *New Mexico*

Quarterly, VI (May, 1936): 123–35. A gathering of comments on and criticisms of *Modern Man* by several of Albuquerque's intellectual and educational leaders (many of whom were personal acquaintances of the author). Interesting, but of little value to the literary critic.

PEARSON, LORENE. "Harvey Fergusson and the Crossroads," *New Mexico Quarterly*, XXI (Autumn, 1951): 334–55. Says the Southwest is "the crossroads of the continent," its tri-ethnic culture giving rise to a "strife between individualism impelling toward devastation and a communalism striving for survival." Claims Fergusson, as time passed, increasingly favored in his books a kind of quirky individualism that was characteristic of the American pioneer. Argues that the writer's works, viewed chronologically, display an overall decline in quality and cogency (a judgment that should be compared with my own very different conclusions).

PILKINGTON, WILLIAM T. "The Southwestern Novels of Harvey Fergusson," *New Mexico Quarterly*, XXXV (Winter, 1965–66): 330–43. Appreciative introduction to the author's regional fiction.

PITTS, REBECCA E. "Where Skies Are Not Cloudy or Gray," *New York Times Book Review*, February 4, 1945, p. 7. Review of *Home in the West*. One of the few sensitive and intelligent reviews of that work. Concludes that "Because of his awareness of the past, and of change, the story of Harvey Fergusson himself is deepened into other dimensions. . . . These suggestive layers of meaning make *Home in the West* a civilized and entertaining addition to our social history."

POWELL, LAWRENCE CLARK. "Books Determine." *Books West Southwest*. Los Angeles: Ward Ritchie Press, 1957. Graceful tribute to Fergusson's Southwestern writings by an enthusiastic commentator on the region's literature. Says the writer's best books are "profoundly conceived, true to life present and past . . . without concessions to Hollywood or to Mrs. Grundy."

———. "*Wolf Song*: Harvey Fergusson." *Southwest Classics*. Los Angeles: Ward Ritchie Press, 1974. An appreciative essay on Fergusson's "classic" novel. Contains useful biographical information on Fergusson.

———. "River Trails." *Southwestern Book Trails: A Reader's Guide to the Heartland of New Mexico and Arizona*. Albuquerque: Horn & Wallace, 1963. Comments on Fergusson's use of the Rio Grande as a unifying element in his works.

ROBINSON, CECIL. "Legend of Destiny: The American Southwest in the Novels of Harvey Fergusson," *The American West*, IV (November, 1967): 16–18, 67–68. Argues that Fergusson, in his historical fiction, employs mythic and legendary aspects of the Southwestern past. Compares the author's fictional explorations of northern New Mexico with Faulkner's utilization of the American South.

————. *With the Ears of Strangers: The Mexican in American Literature.* Tucson: University of Arizona Press, 1963. Survey of Fergusson's use of Mexican-American characters and customs in his writings (see especially pp. 75–94, 101–05). Thorough and perceptive.

TINKLE, LON. "Commerce Comes to Mexico," *Saturday Review,* XXXVII (July 3, 1954): 14. Review of *The Conquest of Don Pedro.* Argues, mistakenly I think, that the novel is an *ironic* study of "the qualities that yield victory: bravery or courage, dedication or discipline, ambition or limitless lust for power." Still, a sympathetic and interesting review. Concludes that Fergusson "is a poet in the way all the best novelists are: he is preoccupied with the intensity and variety of immediate experience."

WHIPPLE, T. K. "The Myth of the Old West." *Study Out the Land.* Berkeley: University of California Press, 1943. Plea for writers to rescue the "Western myth" from fact-grubbing historians and invest it with artistic meaning. Believes that Fergusson attempted such a feat, though the novelist never fully "cut loose and soared like one of his old-timers on a yarn-spinning spree."

WICKENDEN, DAN. "Long Ago, and Far Away," *New York Herald Tribune Book Review,* June 27, 1954, pp. 1, 12. Review of *The Conquest of Don Pedro.* Asserts that there is enough material in the book for a thousand-page historical romance, but that Fergusson economized admirably. Says that the author "never raises his voice; and the very quietness of his writing makes it the more telling." High praise, combined with good analysis of the novel. Many of Wickenden's comments could be applied, with equal justice, to all of Fergusson's historical fiction.

Index